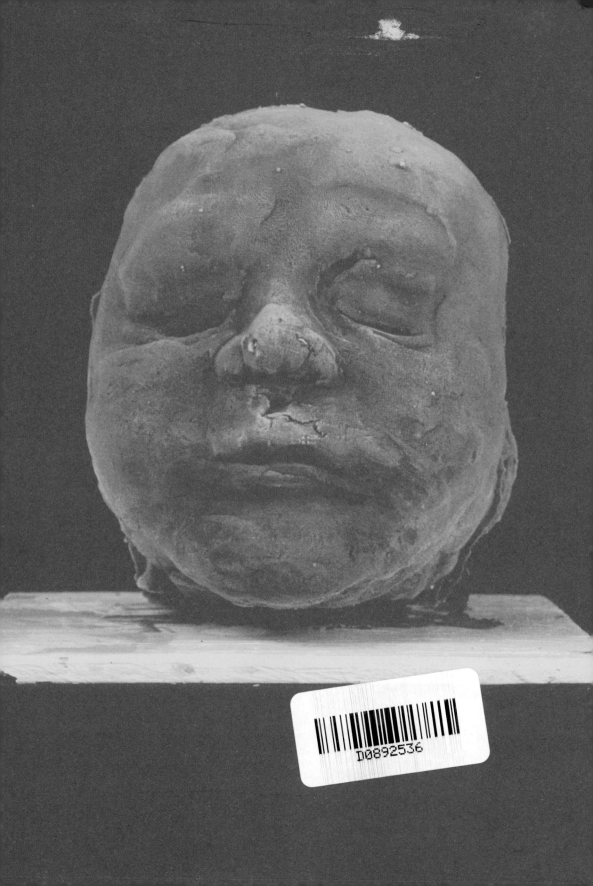

NLA 6/03

Marc Quinn first came to prominence as a sculptor in the early 1990s. His practice, however, has always encompassed a wide range of media that includes painting, drawing, photography and installation to explore issues surrounding the human body, mortality, beauty, science and time. Quinn's insistence on working with his own body is a quest to understand what it physically means to exist in the world. Over the last few years, he has delved deeper into enigmas of the human condition through the representation of other bodies in materials as traditional as marble as well as through the exploration of the essence of life through the use of DNA and blood. While he has become more ambitious in his use of technology, he continues to reference traditional art historical genres such as portraiture, landscape and the still life.

Marc Quinn's work is well known to audiences in Britain and yet there have been few opportunities to see a significant body documenting the diversity of his artistic practice. This exhibition brings together a substantial amount of recent and new work which is presented alongside drawings and photographs from the past decade. This is the first time that a large number of his works on paper have been shown, revealing the critical role of drawing in the creative process for Quinn.

09048868

Published to coincide with the exhibition at Tate Liverpool, this book chronicles Quinn's most recent work and also gives some indication of his thoughts and working processes. We are very grateful to Sarah Whitfield for her insightful questions which formed the starting point for a number of conversations with Marc over the past few months. In this interview Quinn talks in some detail about the different bodies of work in the exhibition and how they are inter-connected yet stand on their own. The publication is designed to act as a handbook, a lexicon of his diverse practice. Our thanks go to the design team at North who have worked closely with Quinn to realise this publication.

Tate Liverpool is indebted to the private collectors who have made their works available for this exhibition. Our thanks also go to Jay Jopling and his staff at White Cube, in particular Irene Bradbury who most generously assisted in the organisation of this exhibition. We are grateful to Chris Miller of Equipment Supplies International Limited for his technical assistance. We are pleased to present a number of Quinn's marble sculptures in the newly renovated Walker in Liverpool and would like to thank Julian Treuherz and Michael Simpson for this fruitful collaboration.

I would also like to thank my colleague Victoria Pomery, until recently Senior Curator at Tate Liverpool. It was a pleasure to collaborate with her on this exhibition, selecting the works and editing this publication.

Lastly, we would like to express our deepest gratitude to Marc Quinn for the enjoyable and inspiring collaboration on the exhibition and publication. Marc expended much energy on both projects while remaining most enthusiastic throughout.

Christoph Grunenberg
Director, Tate Liverpool

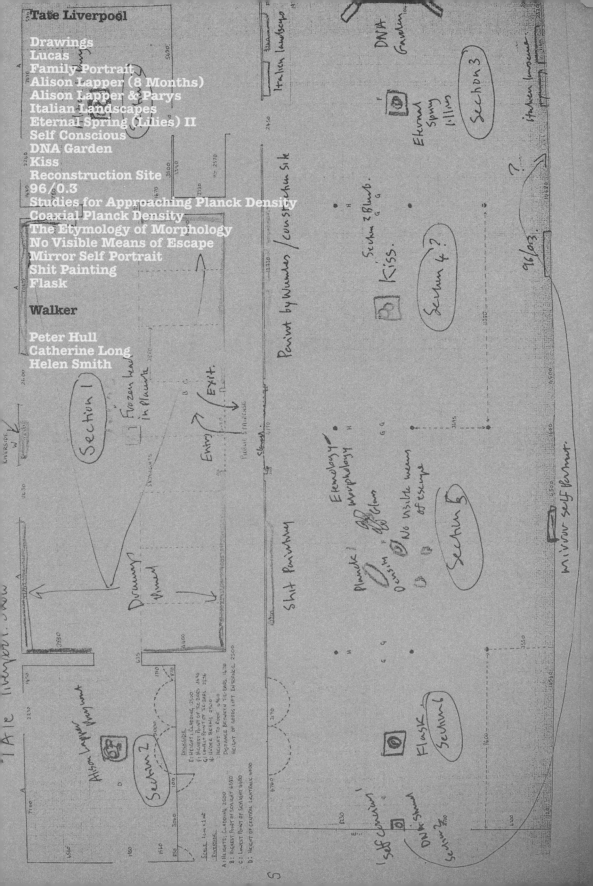

Tate Liverpool

Drawings
Lucas
Family Portrait
Alison Lapper (8 Months)
Alison Lapper & Parys
Italian Landscapes
Eternal Spring (Lilies) II
Self Conscious
DNA Garden
Kiss
Reconstruction Site
96/0.3
Studies for Approaching Planck Density
Coaxial Planck Density
The Etymology of Morphology
No Visible Means of Escape
Mirror Self Portrait
Shit Painting
Flask

Walker

Peter Hull
Catherine Long
Helen Smith

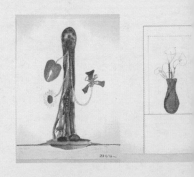

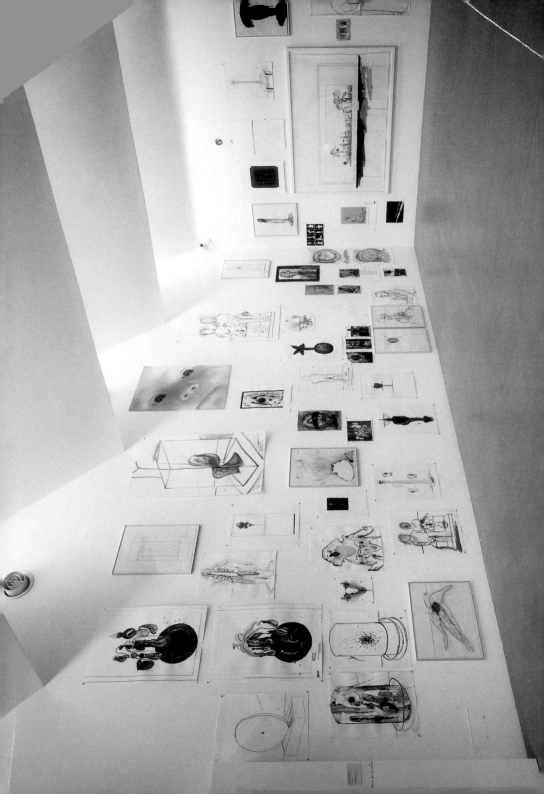

1989 – 2002
Selection of approx.
150 drawings and C-type prints
Dimensions variable
Various media
Courtesy of the artist and Jay
Jopling/White Cube, London

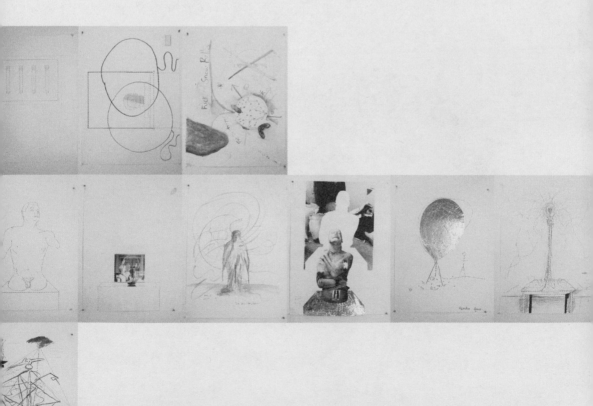

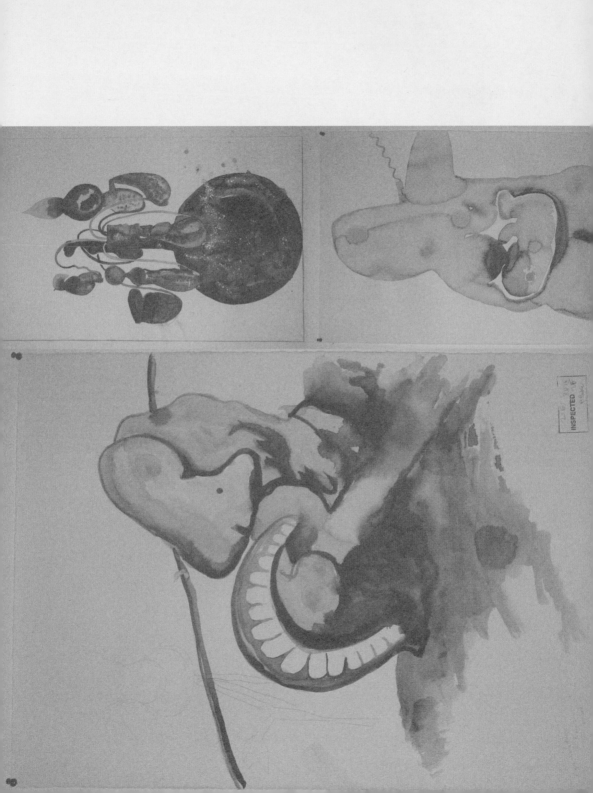

Free Admission:
Marc Quinn talks to Sarah Whitfield
[1] Wall of Drawings

Sarah Whitfield — You begin the exhibition with dozens, possibly hundreds of drawings, watercolours, rough sketches and photographs, some of which are very recent, others date back ten years or so. It's an installation that seems to be very much about beginnings.

Marc Quinn — There are drawings, frozen flowers, babies, Egyptian sculptures, family photographs, etc. I like the idea of showing how things come about, so this room is a mixture of ideas that became sculptures and ideas that never became sculptures, and what's interesting to me is the mixture of the two.

The works are hung as they might be in your studio, that is to say, in no apparent order, and as you have made a point of not labelling them, it's not easy to tell which images became sculptures and which were put aside. Presumably there are ideas here that haven't yet been taken beyond the first stages but which may be realised in the future?

Who knows? Some of the ideas led to others, which eventually superceded them. It's interesting how ideas evolve. I work with mulling ideas, representing them in drawings, and then seeing if after a while these drawing still have a resonance. You question what you've made and that questioning leads you to criticise, and the aspect you criticise most is the one you go on to develop. Asking questions is the only way I can continue to work as an artist, and I like questions that don't have answers but which can be asked in a million different ways. I come up with what people call ideas, but they are not ideas, they are questions.

In the middle of the room is one small sculpture – the head of your son, Lucas, at the age of three days. There seems to be a very strong connection between this and the working material on the walls. As an artist you are dependent upon a store of ideas and found images, just as a baby is dependent upon its parents. That dependency comes across very strongly because the Lucas head is a frozen sculpture which needs a continual supply of electricity.

I see the two parts to this room as equivalents, so that the emergence of the baby is like the emergence of ideas in drawings for works. Of course, the difference is that the baby will go on and become a person, whereas some of the drawings will wither on the vine. It's more like a rainforest. You have all these plants growing and some will become dominant and take over and some of them will just drop away. I wanted it to be about the process of coming to an idea and not just the record of a finished process.

Are you making a connection between the hidden process going on inside the artist's mind and the hidden process going on inside the mother's womb?

That's correct. It's like a womb-room. Put it this way. The step from a drawing to a sculpture is a transformation of information in the same way that the step from the parents to a child is a transformation of information. Something else gets created. *Family Portrait (Cloned DNA)*, which is also shown in this room, makes another connection, this time between the biological and the social. It is a single mirrored frame with four plates of DNA,

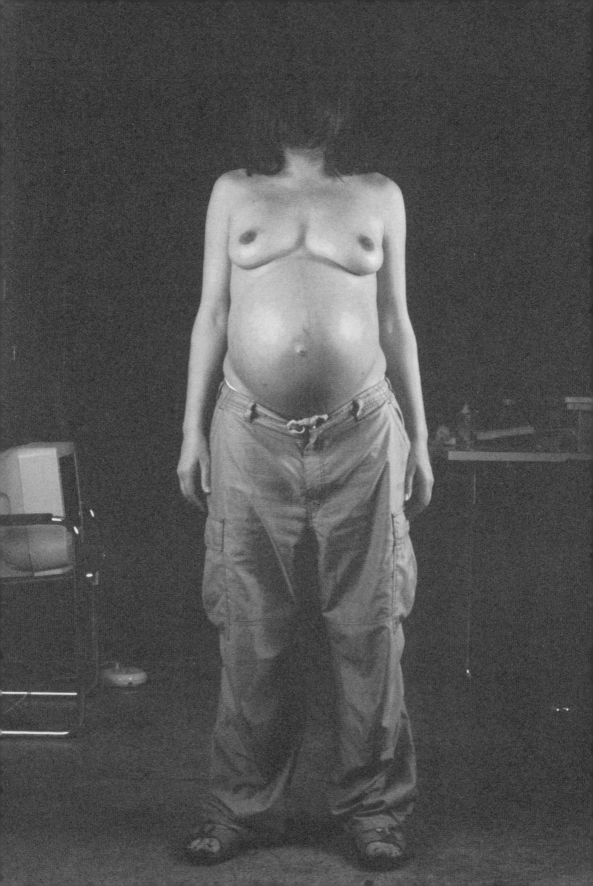

taken from me, my girlfriend, our son Lucas and my step-daughter. That work is about how love can be stronger than biology.

Previous frozen sculptures included self-portraits made out of your own blood. Lucas's head is cast in placenta, which of course is mostly blood. And his head is modelled not cast.

When I made the *Self* sculptures they were life casts, and in a sense the life cast is the most photographic way of doing a portrait; it's the least interpretative, it's the blankest way. But with Lucas's head I was interested in the idea of emergence. In the same way as through drawings the identity of a work will eventually emerge. Who is this baby? He has emerged from his mother's body, but there is also the emergence of his personality. When you first see a baby it becomes itself, but that is not immediate. It's a bit like seeing a flower blossoming. The fact that I modelled the head was really my interpretation of him – of getting to know him.

A baby's head is physically sculpting itself. The plates are all soft and every day the head is changing shape. In a sense, he's making a sculpture of himself. The fact that it's cast in placenta comes from the idea of his separation from his mother's body and becoming himself. At what point does he become an independent baby, no longer a parasite on the maternal body? The placenta is a material meeting point between the two – is it part of the mother's body or part of the baby's, or both? Philosophically, it's an interesting moment. Technically, I don't know the answer, although it must be the child's as the blood from the umbilical cord can be used as a stem cell for him, so he is in a situation with a circulatory system outside his body as well as inside. The miracle, the amazing miracle of a whole-formed person emerging from someone's body is something I can never get over. And yes, dependency is very much an aspect of the sculpture. You have to keep it plugged in. It brings out that side more strongly than the blood head did. A baby is the most dependent thing, and here it is on a life support system. It's like a baby in an incubator...

...or in a womb?

The flex looks like an umbilical cord.

Yes. And even if that analogy seems almost too obvious it's a comment on the way we live in our world. We are so dependent on things we take for granted. We are completely dependent creatures.

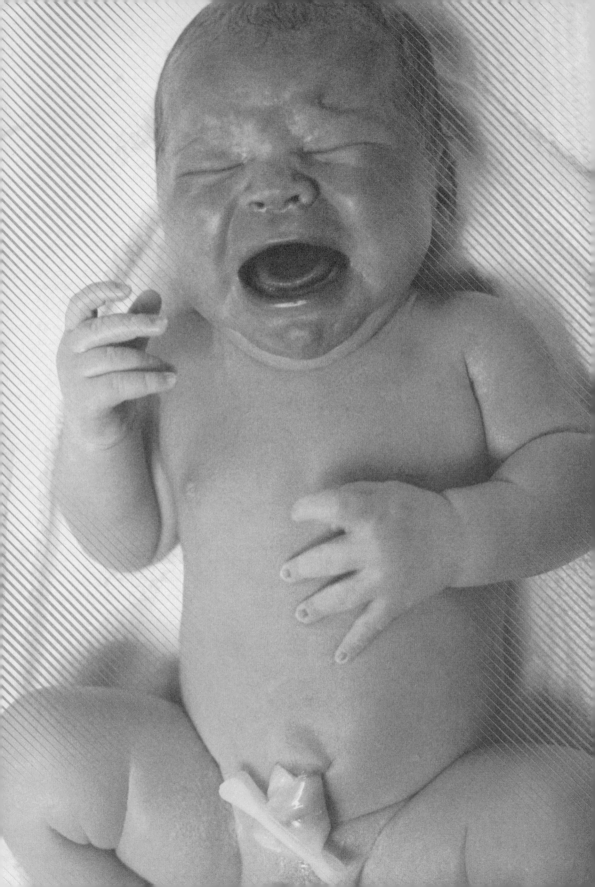

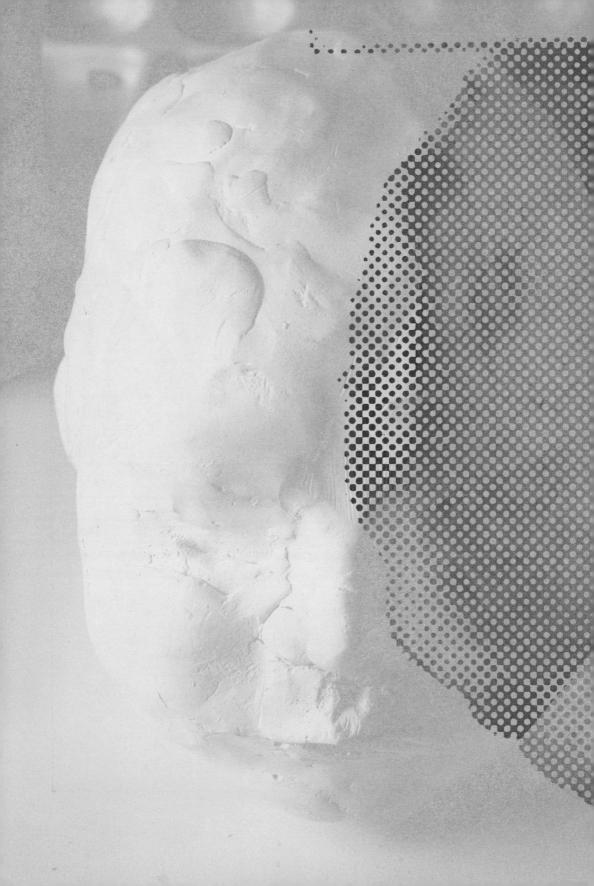

Lucas
2002
2045 x 640 x 640
Human placenta and umbilical
cord, stainless steel, perspex,
refrigeration equipment
Jay Jopling/White Cube, London

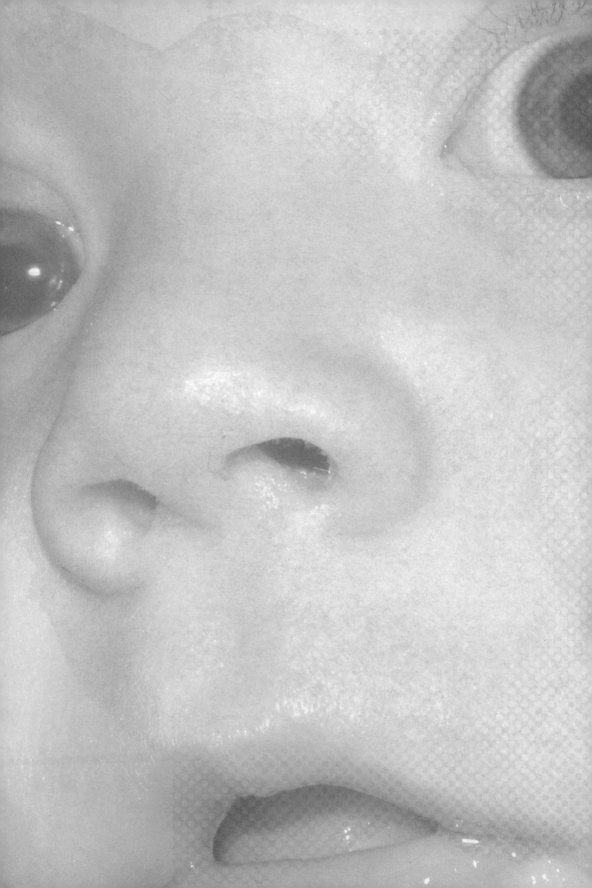

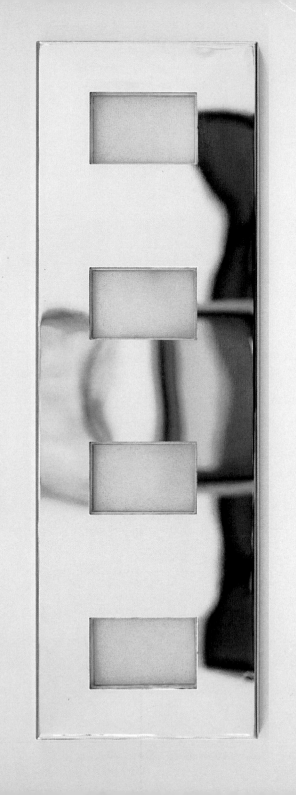

Family Portrait (Cloned DNA)
2002
262 x 205 x 27
Stainless steel, polycarbonate agar
jelly, bacteria colonies, cloned
human DNA
Jay Jopling/White Cube, London

PLANCK DENSITY	BLOOD FLASK / FLOWER	MIRROR	SELF CONSCIOUS

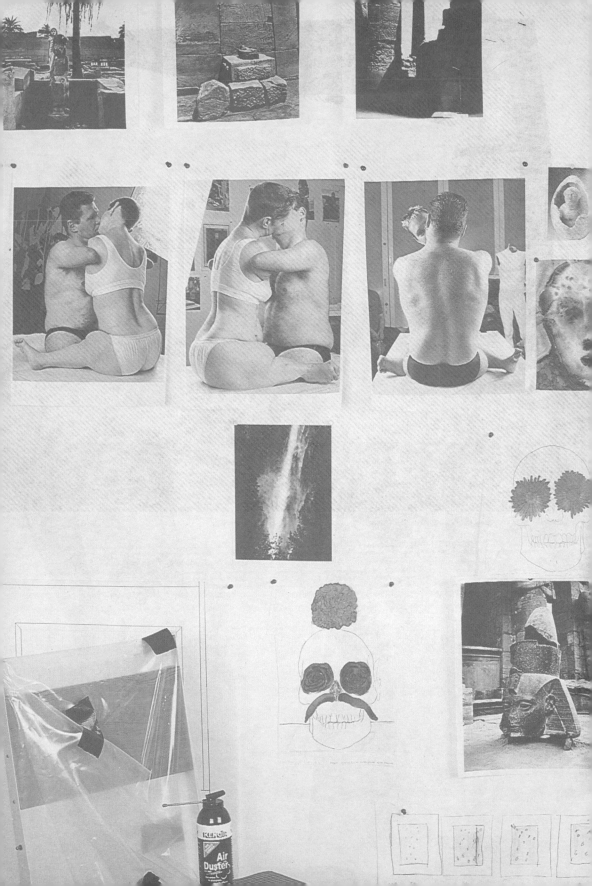

Alison Lapper (8 Months)
2000
335 x 400 x 650
Marble
Mugrabi Collection

Alison Lapper & Parys
2000
835 x 435 x 620
Marble
Mugrabi Collection

Sarah Whitfield — Nowadays, making life-size figures out of a material as traditional as marble seems a high-risk act for a sculptor. What persuaded you to do it?

Marc Quinn — I'll often try and find a medium that's the most devalued and least thought of because that's usually the area in which you can find out how to re-develop something. I'd been thinking about marble, and how to make a marble sculpture that wasn't going to be sucked in by every other marble sculpture. It was only when I saw the fragmented sculptures in the British Museum and the people looking at them that I realised that the reaction of the visitors would be the exact opposite if you had a real person like that. I thought of using the weight of the tradition to undermine itself, although it's not really undermining, it's more like judo – when you use your opponent's strength to turn them over. So, you use the viewer's perception of what a fragmented marble sculpture is to make them feel they know what they are going to look at. As they get closer they can see they are whole people and not fragments. They have to question their ideas of wholeness and fragmentation. In other words, the sculpture is pretending to be one thing but on closer inspection it turns out to be something altogether different.

When you began making the life-size marble sculptures you had eight or more sitters, all men and women who had either been born with physical disabilities or who had suffered amputations through accidents or illness. Did you feel involved in their perception of themselves?

Very much. Even though Peter Hull's body seems fragmented, when he closes his eyes he feels as whole as you or me. Another sitter, Alex Westmoquette, wrote to me saying that it was the most positive thing she'd done since her accident. And in some way, to accept your body and see it celebrated in a material traditionally associated with perfection and with beauty is important. For me, it's an essential part of the sculptures. Even though they came from a conceit about fragmentation they become about wholeness and humanity.

In one of the new sculptures, you seem to be making a deliberate allusion to Rodin's *The Kiss*, a marble sculpture that is very much associated with a conventional idea of physical perfection. Yes, absolutely. It's a kind of updated version, but it's more optimistic. The ideal of a kiss doesn't depend on what the ideal body is. Seeing *Kiss* in the same space as the paintings of plants is a reminder of how things grow, and how genetically dependent we all are. It is also a reminder that we are not totally shaped by our genes, and there is free will.

Your sculpture often makes tough technical demands involving the skills of others as well as your own. How involved are you in the making of these marble sculptures?

Well, I begin by making a plaster cast of the model, and I then go through the cast with the Italian stone carvers in Pietrasanta making detailed notes. It's like printing a programme which can be changed at different points. A point within a circle means bring it up more, a point without a circle means push it in more. They then transfer the thousands of points to the stone and cut it down to within a centimetre of the finished surface, so it's like a 'Michelin Man' version of the sculpture, and then we meet again and go through it with a fine toothcomb. It's a long process which I oversee at every stage.

It's also a process that ensures that none of that intensive labour is visible in the finished sculptures.

Well, yes, the impression you get is that they have arrived fully formed. Other works of mine are about process but these are about the absence of process. I don't like to show hard work on my sleeve. I prefer it to do what it has to do.

The colour of the marble, which is of an almost blinding whiteness, plays up to the perfection of the fully formed look.

I wanted the one you think of as Platonic marble – the whitest. 99% of marble statues aren't pure white – they're yellow, or they have lines running through them. But this marble, which comes from Macedonia, is like the idea of marble. It's even bad taste, beautiful in a way that's almost nauseating. There are little reflective lights in it, like the surface of a sugar mouse. I didn't want it to look like Rodin or Michelangelo where you get the sense of a form emerging from the stone. I wanted it to be absolutely clean, to be super-real, hyper-real. In fact, they are so realistic that ultimately they are unreal.

I know I'm not alone in finding these sculptures among your most difficult works. That may be because we are conditioned to see marble as a very outdated material, but as you say, that's part of its attraction for you. And there's also the subject matter which has led to at least one critic calling you 'smug and exploitative'.

The review you are referring to also criticised the marble sculptures for being such a simple idea. When I read that I thought 'Yes! You've got it!, but you still don't understand it.' The whole point is that it is a simple idea. That's what's good about it. If that moment of assimilation isn't quick and unquestioning then I don't think you shift perceptions in any way, or have any effect. You can't get under the skin. But it's always interesting to read a review like that, just to see how the work can be misinterpreted and to find out if there's any truth in it. I don't think there was in this particular case, though.

I suppose that by calling an idea 'simple' that critic was really saying that there is nothing more clichéd than a kiss and nothing more hackneyed than a marble sculpture?

And bringing the two together is the ultimate challenge. A cliché is a really good subject that has become degraded and can therefore be reinvented. It's become a cliché because it's a very powerful theme or subject, like a mother and child, or a kiss. It's like a beautiful building that has been left to go derelict, and if you do it up, or redevelop it you can make something fantastic. Each generation has to reinvent the cliché because there are only a certain number of themes in the world anyway and it's all about reinventing it in your own time.

One cliché you seem to be reinventing is the heroic monument. Each sitter has the quiet assurance and self-confidence we expect from men and women immortalised in stone.

Certainly. Heroes in ancient times went out and conquered worlds. Heroes nowadays conquer themselves. And they conquer public opinion?

They conquer

public opinion, yes. The *Alison* sculptures, for instance, dare you to ask the unaskable questions. Who's the father? How did she get pregnant? How did she have the baby? Alison was telling me that when she was out shopping near her home one day, she heard two old women muttering behind her 'they shouldn't be allowed to have children'. These are real prejudices that exist in society now and these sculptures might help blow them away – using beauty to conquer prejudice.

Italian Landscape 10
2000
1098 x 1663 x 42
Permanent pigment on canvas
White Cube

Italian Landscape 5
2000
1098 x 1663 x 42
Permanent pigment on canvas
Jay Jopling/White Cube, London

Italian Landscape 3
2000
1098 x 1663 x 42
Permanent pigment on canvas
Jay Jopling/White Cube, London

Italian Landscape 6
2000
1098 x 1663 x 42
Permanent pigment on canvas
Jay Jopling/White Cube, London

[3] Eternal Spring (Lilies) II

Sarah Whitfield — Before moving on to *Eternal Spring*, the frozen flower sculpture, can we talk about the freezing process itself? In 1991 you had the idea of freezing a mould of your own head using nine pints of your own blood. You obviously had to master the technical side of making this kind of sculpture. How difficult was that?

Marc Quinn — The idea itself is simple. I made a mould of my head, had the freezer made and poured the blood in. But then I found that because the head was unsealed, the cold air blowing around it was dehydrating it. If I had left it like that it would have freeze-dried and turned into a pile of powder. I had unwittingly built a freeze-drying machine, so then I was on a fast-track learning curve to learn how to deal with this. The problem was that the head was on public display at the time, so we had to try out all sorts of barrier sprays and creams, and it was pretty much a nightmare.

No. I have a technical mind. I was a boy who built things out of Meccano™ or electrical bits and pieces. I have a technical side I can rely on. And I usually find that if you talk to an expert and ask the right questions you can essentially find out as much as they can, and often see things that they miss. In any case, I was able to use the freeze-drying method in a positive way later by making the ice-sculptures that evaporated.

I realised I needed a barrier between the head and the refrigerating air. I talked to my father, who is a scientist and various other people and realised that silicone is an inert and colourless liquid which has the quality of staying liquid down to minus eighty degrees centigrade. It's ideal because you can pour it frozen and it doesn't chemically attack or penetrate what is put in it. That solved the head. And then I thought what is the most delicate, ethereal thing? A flower. What would happen if you put a flower into a vat of frozen silicone?, and that was the initial idea for the flower sculptures.

If they degenerate, the work becomes pointless. It's about the illusion of perfection, about the impossible dream, about immortality.

When an earlier work *White Lilies* was shown I kept putting the flowers in the silicone and they kept going brown. Everything was so rushed and I couldn't work it out because I had one in the bench freezer in the studio that had been there for six months and was perfect. Eventually I realised that you have to keep UV light away from them, so now they have to be shown in a controlled lighting environment.

I can't say. All I know is that there's a flower in my freezer and it's been there since 1996 and it's perfect. Working on these pieces is a bit like working on the space shuttle programme. The whole thing can blow up because one kind of rubber used in a gasket went hard when it got cold instead of going soft and started a series of chain reactions. So each time you build a new sculpture you never know which tiny detail will throw the whole thing, so you have to experiment. But that's very difficult because essentially I'm trying to run a research and development programme with no investment apart from my own, and no time. And lots of people wanting things immediately.

Do you enjoy working under that sort of pressure?

I think I must do. *Flask II*, for example, is turning out to be an absolute nightmare to make. But that's the way we live. We are very dependent. If our environment was not exactly right it would be a disaster...

...which sounds like the human condition

...exactly. That's why I like the flower sculptures. They make that explicit. They have some sense of being alive because they live in a condition that could just disappear within a second. They are about the thin line between life and death, I suppose, and the dependence on so many things to maintain that.

You talk about a thin line, but the flower sculptures are really about that line, aren't they?

They are both, and they are one. The flowers are dead but they appear to be alive. Immaculate perfection always evokes revolting death and decay to me. The flower sculptures make that very explicit. Their perfection is really a dead thing and if you turn the freezer off decay sets in, but of course when the rotting begins it is life reasserting itself. It's as though you find the point at which beauty is pushed to its absolute limits. One artist you remind me of very strongly is Bonnard, who was fascinated by extremes of ripeness, by the moment at which ripeness turns to decay.

I think so. I like things that throw you between polarities, sometimes you see it one way, sometimes the other. What I like about the frozen flowers is that they appear to be untransformed, but in fact they are utterly transformed. You can say that they are a sculpture of a flower made from the same material as the flower. But the transformation happens without one realising it, before one's very eyes. For me sculpture is about transformation.

And what about your choice of flower for *Eternal Spring*? The lily carries such a weight of association as a symbol of purity, in paintings of the Annunciation, for example.

I'd seen the flower in so many paintings and it has a kind of vestigial figurative aspect, which I liked. I also liked the fact that whiteness is the colour that is fastest to disappear, the one that is most vulnerable to decay. I was trying to choose the ultimate in delicacy...

And perfection, even though perfection isn't perfect. And perfection is not really the ultimate goal. The Calla lily is a flower that is strangely artificial. It's like a sculpture. It is as though it has evolved according to desire rather than according to nature, though it's easy to forget that evolution is really the history of desire.

Eternal Spring (Lilies) II
1998
2197 x 900 x 900
Stainless steel, glass,
frozen silicone, lilies, refrigeration
equipment
Private Collection, London

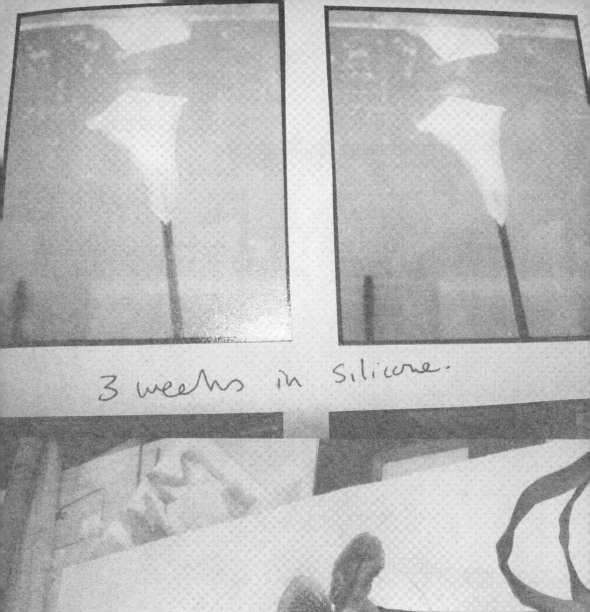

3 weeks in silicone.

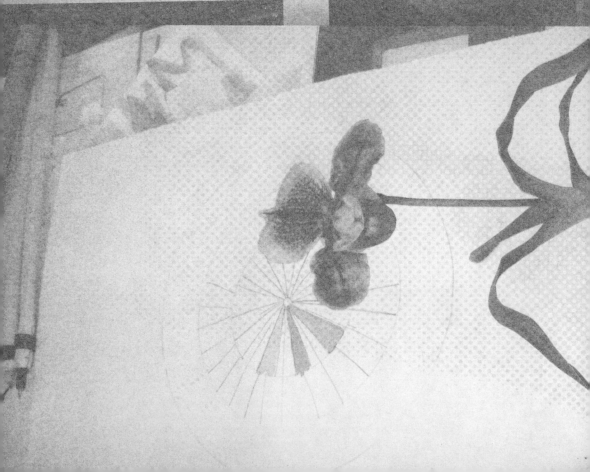

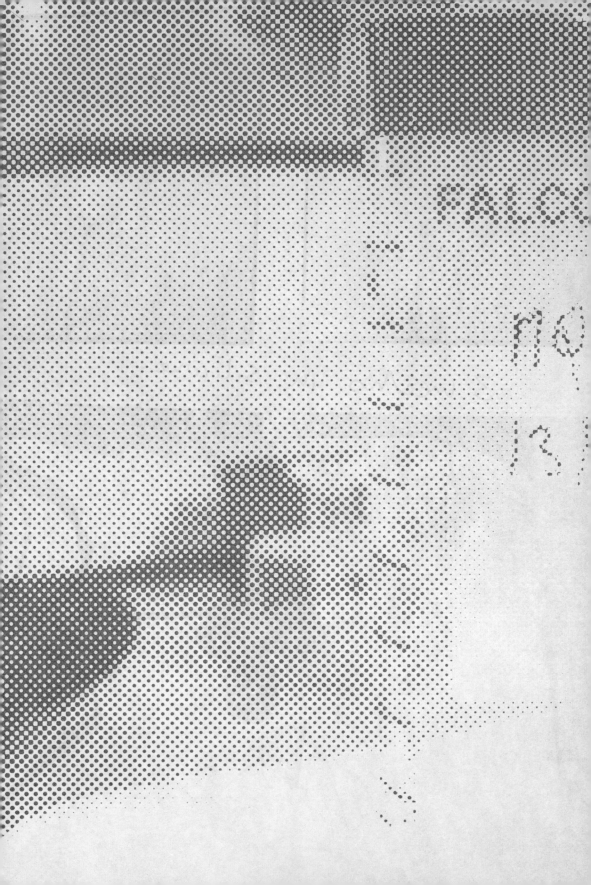

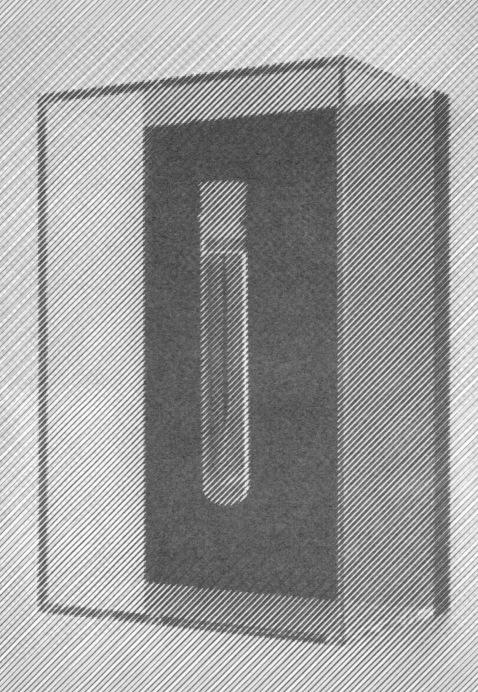

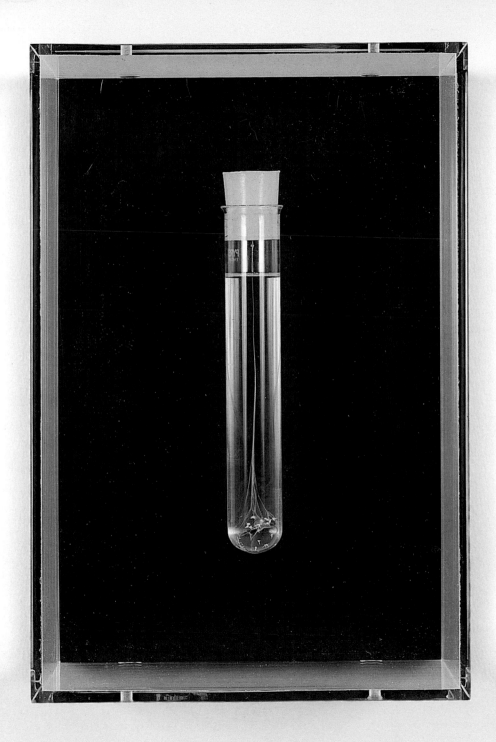

Self Conscious
2000
190 x 120 x 275
Glass, perspex, 90% alcohol
and human DNA (Artist's)
Collezione Prada

DNA Garden
2002
1925 x 3260
Stainless steel frame, polycarbonate agar jelly, bacteria colonies, 77
plates of cloned DNA – 75 plants, 2
humans
Jay Jopling/White Cube, London

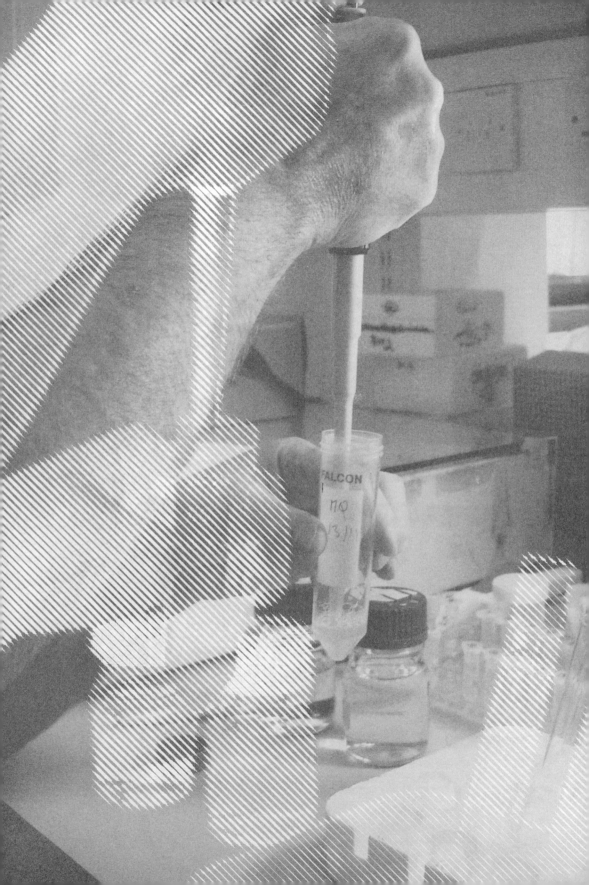

[4] Garden of Eden

Marc Quinn —
This piece is a literalization of the Garden of Eden because if
you follow back the DNA of all the plants and the two human
beings there will be a point where they converge, and that
will be some single cell amoeba which is the Garden of Eden.
What's interesting to me is that reality should be the real stuff
and not illustrated. I always think that the literal is much
more ambiguous than anything else. You get to a different
reality. It's like science. The more you find out the more
there is to find out.

I thought it
was a sculpture but I didn't realise it wasn't until I saw what
the real sculptural solution might be.

The work had become like an old bone I was gnawing
away at. There was something about the flat plane that wasn't
working and I couldn't understand why. And then when we
took it to the fabricator he said it was very difficult to get one
sheet of metal that size to fit through the polishing machine
so that made me think of making it in two or three sections.
At the time I was reading a book on Hieronymus Bosch and
I realised that this was what I had been looking for. It had to
be in three sections like *The Garden of Earthly Delights* with
the two side panels folding in like shutters. I have always
loved the transparent sphere reflecting the world which is on
the back of the side panels of the Bosch painting, and my way
of expressing that is to mirror the back of the side panels of
DNA Garden.

Exactly. Science has become the religion of now,
and I like the idea of preservation and protection that comes
from being able to close the panels. It's a safe, and it's also a
library. Technically that is what a thread of DNA is called – a
library. You open a library of DNA to make the plates with the
bacteria, so the seventy-seven petri dishes are the equivalent
of books. From one 'library' you can make thousands of books.

DNA is so beautiful. It's like
the thread of life. Even before I made this work the delicacy
of DNA reminded me of the transparent sphere on the back of
Bosch's painting. These are just my poetical projections on to

it but it's more interesting in reality than the idea of it. Things are never how you imagine them to be. Everything has a poetry to it in some way. Even the most pared down thing.

Their physical scale reminds me of early Netherlandish portraits, and also Daguerreotypes because they are a kind of biological photograph, a photograph back through a vertiginous tunnel of time. You are fixing a part of a person through a chemical process. It's not an image of them but it is a part of them. But the scale is also enormous. In the DNA thread in *Self-Conscious* there are ten million copies of my complete human genome and in one of the little petri dishes with the bacteria colonies a three-thousandth of those ten million contain the same amount of information, so your whole sense of scale completely disappears. Scale is a very sculptural concept and here you have a reality that throws it completely.

Well, they don't need a life support system, but they are dependent on the fact that the plate containing them is sealed and that the agar jelly in which the bacteria holding the DNA is suspended won't dehydrate. If you broke the seal the jelly would dry out. Basically it's like a body, it needs to be kept hydrated, like a skin.

It's interesting that you see tactility without touching – you can sense material with your eyes. I always think of these DNA works as a piece of skin that has been cut out and preserved in some way, like a precious object or a holy relic. And the way I present them is a part of that.

So what are we talking about? The DNA works are relics, they are like traditional saints' relics.

Kiss
2002
1759 x 640 x 600
Marble
Jay Jopling/White Cube, London

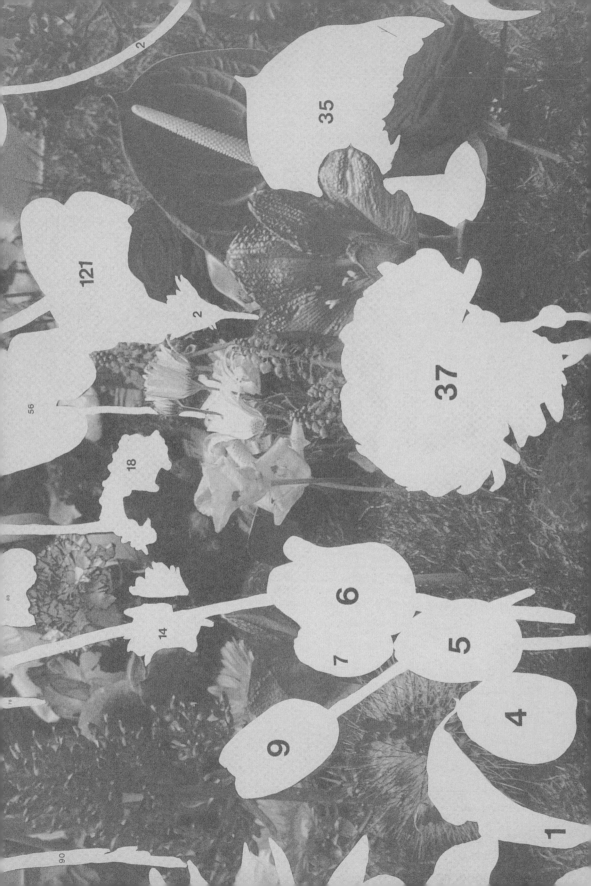

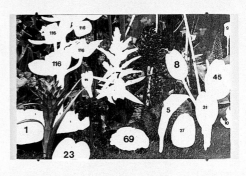

Painting by Numbers
2000
1098 x 1663 x 42
Permanent pigment, acrylic
and letraset on canvas
Jay Jopling/White Cube, London

Reconstruction Site
2001
1100 x 1660 x 50
Canvas, permanent pigment,
acrylic and letraset
Jay Jopling/White Cube, London

Reconstruction by Numbers
2001
1110 x 1656 x 50
Canvas, permanent pigment,
acrylic and letraset
Jay Jopling/White Cube, London

Reconstruction
2001
1100 x 1660 x 50
Canvas, permanent pigment,
acrylic and letraset
Jay Jopling/White Cube, London

Sarah Whitfield — 96/0.3, the painting of your grandmother holding your baby son, is based on a photograph that started out as just another family photo. What made you decide to turn it into a work?

Marc Quinn — Sometimes a drawing or a photograph can transform themselves in front of your eyes. I just printed the roll out and left one of the prints on the office wall. When I came in to the studio the next day it was just shouting at me that it was a work and not just another family snapshot. I suddenly recognised themes in it that were interesting and relevant. It's the oldest person and the youngest, the beginning and the end. And I like my grandmother's understanding, her acceptance of her position on the spectrum of age. It's like a Renaissance Madonna and Child, but not like it because whereas all art is metaphor there's something about a photograph that's real. It's a real picture and a real moment, yet it has a sense of an archetypal image. In a sense, it's a ready-made.

But you didn't want to leave the photograph just as it was?

I've always kept away from colour photography because of its fugitiveness – a colour photograph lasts somewhere between thirty and forty years. I want things to be fugitive when I want them to be but not when I don't want them to be. And then I started to work with Adam Lowe who had been re-inventing some of the early colour photography methods from the 1930s and 40s, including carbo-prints which are pigment transfer. You take the image and transfer them to layers of pigment rather than dye, and pigments are painting and if you choose the right ones they never fade. I call them paintings because they are like a contemporary way of making a permanent image, like Warhol used screenprinting, for example. It was like freezing flowers but in a different way.

You keep coming back to the question of permanence.

I'm making art for people now and for myself, but I'm also making work someone will look at in five hundred years time, perhaps, when people may get something completely different from it. They're all messages in bottles, aren't they?

Sometimes you mix photography and painting as in Painting by Numbers, a series that relates to The Garden. Do the numbers have anything to do with the varieties you used in that work?

No, they don't. I wanted it to be more ambiguous. We are surrounded by numbers. Their randomness and our inability to understand what they are is important. I wanted it to be about the manipulation of nature as well. There is no such thing as nature anymore. It's all culture now. Every landscape you see is a manipulated landscape, every flower has been genetically modified through breeding to be like it is, so these pictures are about The Garden being constructed not grown, that's one aspect. They are also about numbers as instructions, as in painting by numbers, a construction map or a genetic diagram. By naming the world you create it, but that's ambiguous because naming and classifying – which I'm quite interested in – is artificial. There is always something compelling in art when it's ambiguous, where there is a space into which you can project yourself. That's when things seem alive.

96/0.3
2002
1538 x 1025
Pigment print on gessoed board
Jay Jopling/White Cube, London

Did all the plants in *The Garden* behave as you expected them to when they were submerged in the frozen silicone?

Not always.

The number 12 refers to the 12 in the darkest of the paintings in this series – a Nepenthes plant, the same plant I used for *Flask*. When we submerged it air became trapped in its base which made it turn upside down, so it's a hidden clue that we are looking at a world that is upside down.

And it's a clue that came about purely by accident?

Exactly. Accident and chance happen all the time, but it's being able to recognise which ones are fruitful that is important.

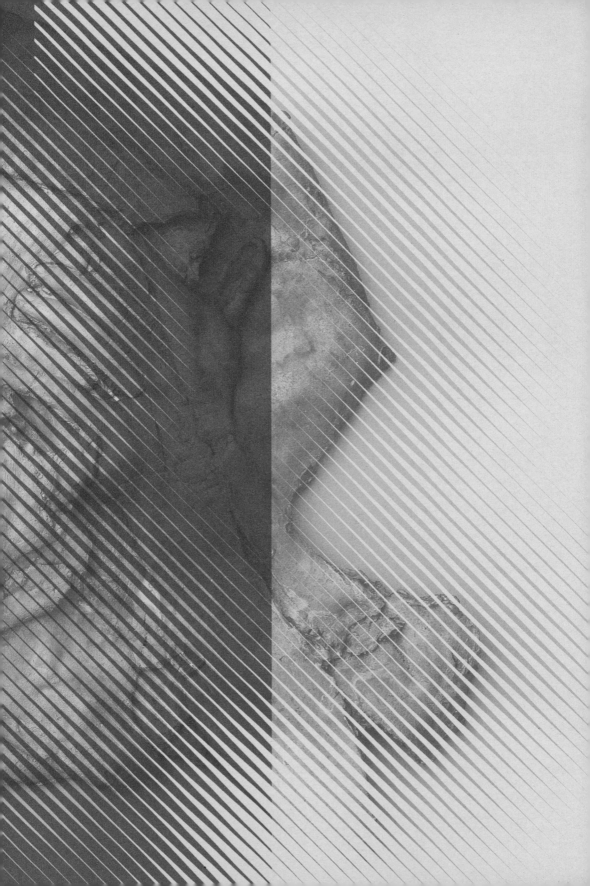

Sarah Whitfield — The title *Planck Density* presumably refers to the German physicist Max Planck?

Marc Quinn — Yes, the Planck Constant is the absolute zero of density and so it just seemed an appropriate title for a work that is about compression, about density and mass and things returning to original matter.

In these works lead is shown to be a highly emotional material in that it seems to express the finality of death even more powerfully than marble or bronze.

What I like about lead is that technically it is a liquid. These sculptures are still in movement, movement that is being caused by gravity. In ten thousand years time they will be flatter and wider and eventually over a long, long time they will become flat pools of lead. They are clocks in a way and they are still moving. So they are articulating in reality what they are illustrating. Gravity is pulling them down but in a way that is too slow for us to see. It's actually happening as well as looking as though it's happening.

They are like *Eternal Spring* in that the act of transformation is invisible. The lilies look alive but are dead, and here the lead looks completely dead but is actually alive, in that it is moving. Moving towards a very slow death. Or returning to another state?

That's it. They don't seem negative to me. They are rather elegiac. Maybe wistful and a little melancholic, but they're peaceful. They remind me of a dressing gown that has been dropped on to the floor, or a pair of trousers that drop to the ground when you undo the belt. And that's what they are in a way. Dropped. I get the wax and mould it myself and put it in a hot bath and then when it's very soft I drop it on the floor and it flattens out. And then when it has gone hard again I cast it in lead. They are not sculptures in the sense that a sculpture is an object that has been frozen, like a marble statue. They are not about the static, they are about softness and about flow, and about time.

That's another innovation, isn't it, using time as a material?

That's a nice way of putting it.

But that is how I feel you do use it.

That is how I use it, but I hadn't actually verbalised it like that.

These sculptures remind me of your description of the pathology experiments in America you read about recently in which bodies are laid out and left to decompose in a field.

That's why when I saw the article in *The New Scientist* I was so excited by it. It was exactly what I had been doing with the *Planck Density* sculptures, only it was a different way of expressing a similar idea.

Here there's no sense of a body rotting. It's just pure matter returning to its natural state, but then I suppose that is what decomposition is.

It's a bit like the idea that when the frozen head melts the imprint of the face disappears and you can't say where it's gone. It has just gone. The body is dissolving, a slow fade out of a human print. The smaller sculptures in the series are

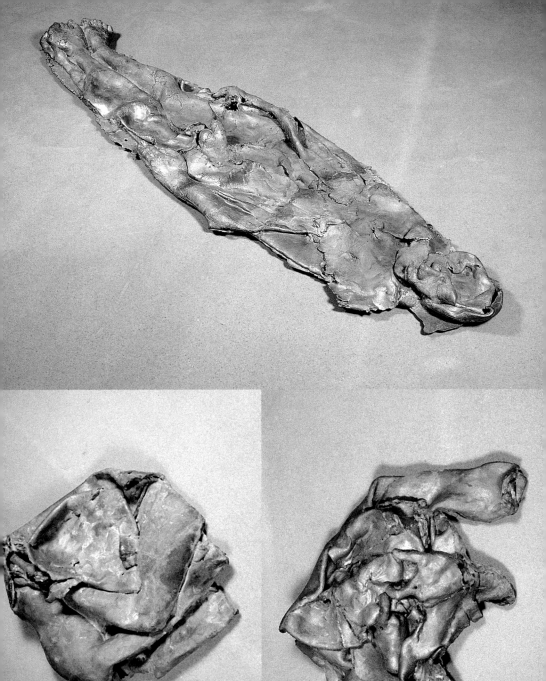

Coaxial Planck Density
1999
1860 x 520 x 120
Cast lead
Jay Jopling/White Cube, London

Study for Approaching Planck
Density 82.75 Kg
1998
570 x 500 x 150
Cast lead
Courtesy of the artist

Study for Approaching Planck
Density 64.5 Kg
1998
670 x 440 x 130
Cast lead
Courtesy of the artist

made from the torsos of the *Detox* series I made in 1994 and 1995 so they are a sort of fast-forward version, in other words, the ones you see here are the *Detox* ones in five thousand years time.

So you've constructed your own time frame?

Exactly.

The choice of material is crucial to the meaning, isn't it?

The material is the reality. It is velvety and soft and I love the colour of it. I also find the flatness very satisfying. The long version of the sculpture looks like a boat, and it also looks like a vagina. It's like a grey version of a large coloured photograph I made of the vagina, only it's a dark echo of it at the other end of life.

Your analogy with a boat links up with the Ancient Egyptians' belief in the journey of the dead across the river *Styx* and, as you say, lead is a liquid so water is already implicit in the material.

Yes, you have the sense of a river or a sea, and a boat taking a form somewhere. I like the idea that nothing lasts forever.

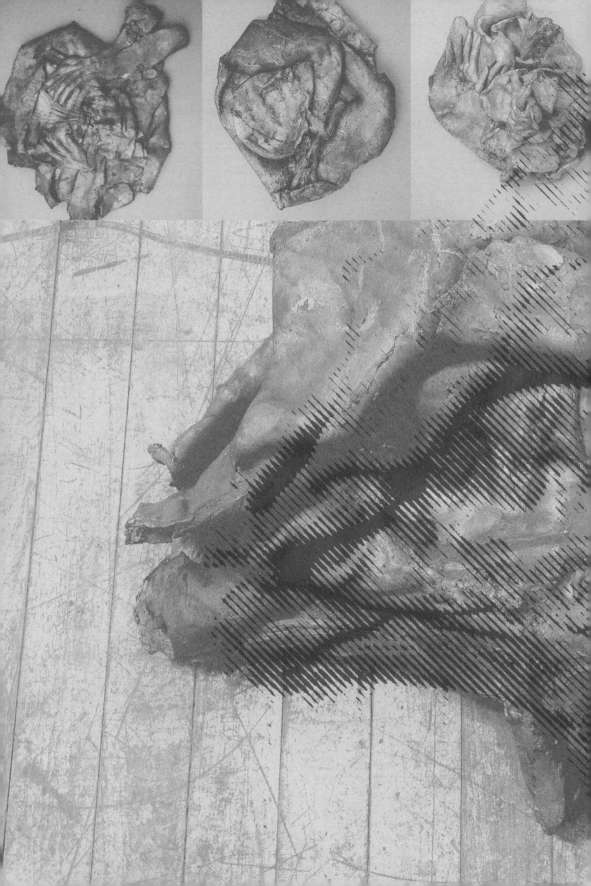

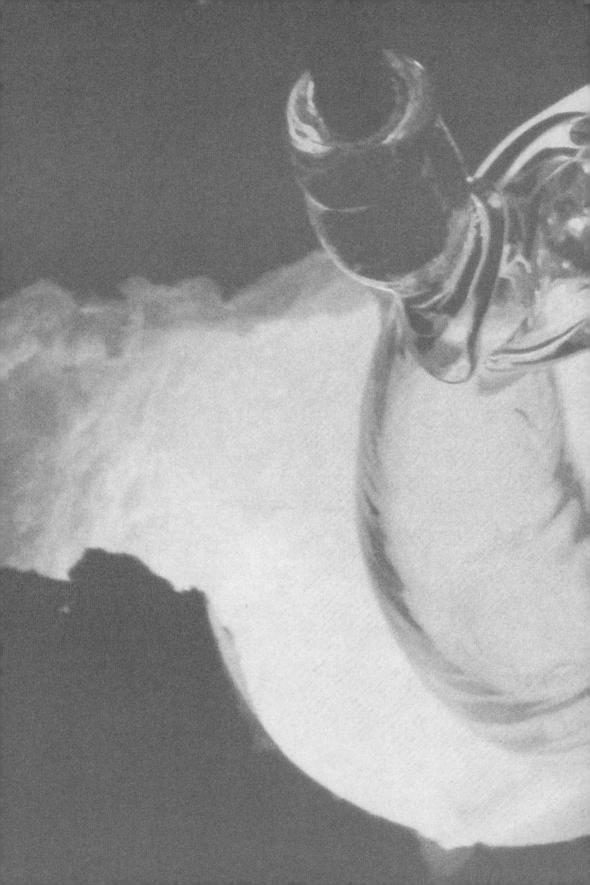

Sarah Whitfield — The sense of movement that is invisible in *Planck Density* is more tangible in *The Etymology of Morphology* as the individual forms that make up the body look as volatile as mercury.

Because it's made from blown glass, it's all one liquid. I see in it the infinite possibilities of every person. It consists of abstract parts and figurative parts such as the head, the hand and the penis – elements that refer to the intellectual life, the manual and the sexual, as well as the things you don't see going through your life, likes genes. And because the pieces are mirrored, they take on any environment you put them into. It reminds me that we sometimes act out things in our lives that we can't see we are doing. There is a genetic imperative making us do things which to us are invisible. It's a companion piece to the Lucas head in that it's about some sort of emergence or birth. But what interests me is that it's a very contemporary image inspired by *The Terminator* films and yet I've made it using a completely old-fashioned material and method. Technically, this sculpture could have been made five hundred years ago.
How are the pieces made?

They are made by glass blowers in Murano who have a flawless grasp of their technique. It's a question of using their strengths to do something different. The pieces are blown in clear glass and then holes are drilled in the base and a craftsman, who silvers mirrors, silvers the inside using silver nitrate. It was created on the hoof, that is, I drew the shapes on a piece of paper and the glass blower created them. It's a record of an improvisation.

When we were talking earlier (off tape) you compared your role in the making of *Etymology* to a director working with actors.

It's a performance, and very theatrical. You are in this large room with a huge furnace and people are dancing around with big bits of glass. There's a specific movement involved, because they have to keep the glass moving all the time, putting it in the furnace, taking it out, putting it in. It's like a dance, and I think that comes across in the work.

The way the separate parts are laid out on the floor, together with the mixture of the figurative and the abstract, seems to catch the Baroque sense of a figure writhing. At the same time, it has a Baroque lightness of touch and playfulness.

It has a celebratory feel. But I like the fact that it is only made with the interaction of human breath and gravity and heat. The whole sculpture is like a breath.

The Etymology
of Morphology
1996
270 x 1525 x 1520
Glass and silver
Tate

Sarah Whitfield — The violence, which is so contained in a work like *Flask*, seems much more explicit in *No Visible Means of Escape*.

Marc Quinn — It's an extreme moment of transformation, a violent shedding of skin. I'm always conscious that everything exists in the dimension of time, so these works are about shedding your past in a sense, and the way in which we are different people all the time. We are constantly transforming ourselves. This is not about the final transformation, when a living being becomes an inert object. These sculptures are not about death. I was thinking more about liberation.

The ripping feels physically violent.

They have the violence of reality, but the violence has come from within, rather than being inflicted upon them. They are like seed pods that have burst open.

Should we see them as a sort of human chrysalis?

Yes. It's like a cocoon that hangs down and something suddenly emerges from it. But the thing about the human chrysalis is that it doesn't alter in shape. You look exactly the same as you did after something in your life has changed, but you have changed. That's not necessarily how these sculptures are viewed but that doesn't matter. I think it's important that each work has its own life.

They are made out of polyurethane, which I suppose is the material that is most like skin?

It has the same texture and feeling of skin, yes, and the softness. It's about being trapped in our bodies, but there is also a liberating side to it. It's escaping from what you have become without realising it. And also escaping from the confines of your boundaries, or your dimensions. Escaping from becoming a sculpture. They are saying that the physical is not the real dimension of a person.

That sense of constriction seems to recur frequently in your work. I don't think it's a point you set out to make, by the way. It just seems to be there, in the frozen flowers, the blood head, even in the DNA pieces.

Well yes, but by evoking constriction I am also evoking the opposite. I like to create a situation that can oscillate between two polarities. The constriction here comes from the sudden realisation that you are in the present moment and that you can be nowhere else. I keep being reminded of something William Burroughs wrote: 'Your body constitutes an almost escape-proof prison. Once you understand that, then you have the possibility of escape.'

You have made several versions of *No Visible Means of Escape*. Is the process always the same?

There are different ways of making them. In this one, for example, I made a complete polyurethane figure, and then I hung it up and got a knife and cut it open, rather like flaying a figure. With others I made the figure in two halves and joined them at the head. This one was beautiful to make sculpturally because as you run your knife down it, the weight of the material causes it to tear and it makes its own form. So there is an element of chance in the transformation of the form, which I like because I haven't completely thought the sculpture out. It helped create itself. When you take on the human body, which is, after all, one of the great themes of art, especially sculpture, are you conscious of making connections with other art, with other times? Yes, absolutely. Making connections is what artists do. Everyone sees his own personal history of art.

And how do you see yours?

Well, Bernini to me is completely about the body as the prison of the soul. The body of *Beata Ludovica Albertoni* is a body trying to transcend itself in some way, through its writhings. The same is true of Bernini's *Ecstacy of Saint Theresa*. On a formal level I love Baroque sculpture, and in a sense *No Visible Means of Escape* is a reinterpretation of Baroque form.

I certainly see a strong connection between the Baroque and your love of extremes. For one thing, there's a shared pleasure in using materials to undermine natural states. Your frozen flower sculptures, for example, which, as you say, are about transformation, remind me very much of Bernini's *Apollo and Daphne* which is all about a moment of transformation.

It's one of my favourite sculptures. It shows how sculpture works in a different way from painting – a painted image of that subject would be nothing like as strong as the experience of it in three-dimensions. It feels like one long exhalation. I love the paradox of taking a very heavy material and making it as light as air.

Going back to *No Visible Means of Escape*, the idea of a suspended sculpture is a particularly modern one. I'm thinking of Eva Hesse, for example....

...or Claes Oldenburg. I remember seeing his *Soft Drainpipe – Blue (Cool)* at the Tate when I was about eight or nine years old. I was very impressed by that. I remember really loving the foldedness of it, and the fact that it makes itself – you pull a rope and the folds create themselves. But that's the formal thing. Those sorts of questions that used to be at the centre of art are not so important anymore. What's interesting to me is to make art that's about reality, not about formal invention. Of course formal invention comes into it, but it's never the primary reason.

But it is a delicate balance between the two?

Yes, but it comes out of the intention. They go hand in hand and it's very difficult to separate them. Formal invention is really about taking joy in working and it's about play. That's what artists are, they are people who are able to play.

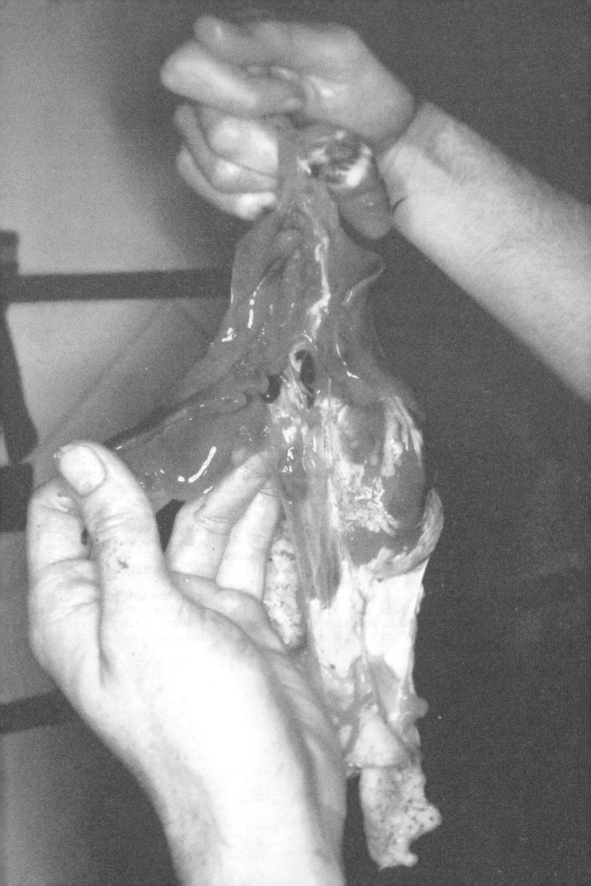

No Visible Means
of Escape IV
1996
4000 x 600 x 400
R.T.V. polyurethane
Tate

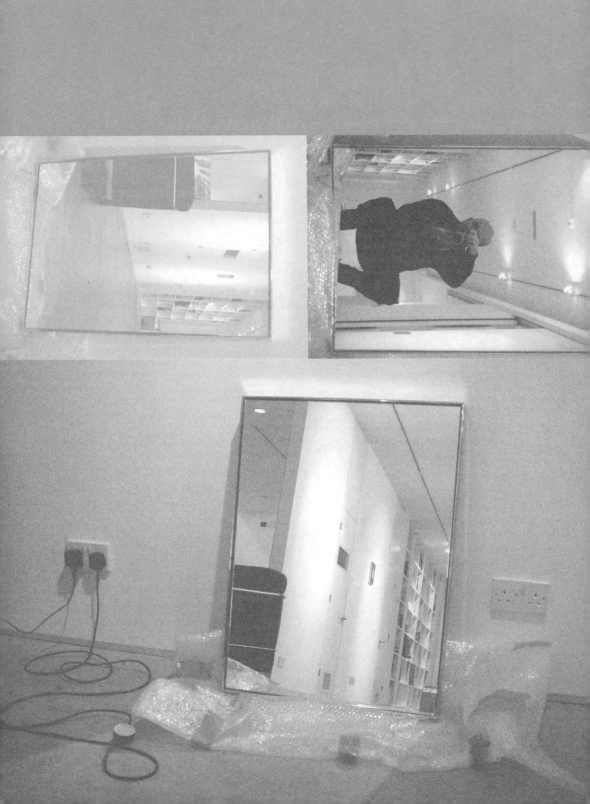

Mirror Self Portrait
2001 – 2002
1988 x 1435
Mirror, stainless steel box frame
Jay Jopling/White Cube, London

Sarah Whitfield — Your *Labyrinth Mirror Self Portrait* looks like a perfectly ordinary mirror. What is so special about it?

Marc Quinn — It's a mirror I have looked into every day for a year. It hangs in the bathroom in the studio. It's an anti-sentimental piece; it's about how matter doesn't have memory. What I love about mirrors is that they are always in the present moment. They are like someone with amnesia, or Karkov's syndrome. It's certainly not about the sort of mumbo-jumbo that says if you look into a mirror long enough a part of you stays inside, or anything like that. It's the opposite. I could look in that mirror for a hundred years and it would still be a mirror. And that's what it's about. We will die and the world will go on.

I can see how the mirror might connect with the DNA works, for example, because it shares the same quality of indifference. I was struck recently by something Richard Dawkins said, 'DNA neither cares nor knows. DNA just is'. To some people that indifference is very frightening.

Absolutely. The mirror is the ultimate indifferent object. It celebrates you while you are there and then when you have gone it forgets you immediately.

You might as well not have been there.

Exactly. And there is also something comforting about it. You don't really have to worry. The whole world isn't on your shoulders. In fact the world doesn't give a shit about your shoulders.

It's also like a viewer who is completely non-judgemental. Wherever you place it, in any exhibition it will be reflecting your work as well as itself.

When you make a work of art and then let it go out into the world, the viewer replaces the artist, and it's what they bring to the work that activates it in some way. In this case, the viewer literally replaces the artist.

And you're a literalist.

Oh yes! I love the literal. And my experience is that the more literal you try to become the more ambiguous the situation gets. There's no such thing as blank literalness. The mirror looks blank but, technically, reflectiveness in metallic surfaces is a mobile sea of electrons. We think of ourselves as solid whereas in fact we are mostly liquid. There are a few dry dusty places but mostly we are water. But because it's a mirrored surface the sculpture continues in the present moment. The surface is constantly of the now. It's alive and that gives it a vitality.

[10] Shit Paintings

Sarah Whitfield — Everything you do has a very clean feel to it. In fact, looking at your work I would guess that you had a horror of mess. And yet, there's nothing messier than shit. Or blood, for that matter.

Marc Quinn — In real life, in natural conditions, I'm a very messy person. My work appears to be controlled but it's a kind of cleaning-up process. You have something that's very messy and it's a question of paring it down until it's reduced to the essential. The *Shit Paintings* are a reminder that we are terribly abstracted from our interiors. We carry around gallons of viscerality and shit and blood and yet here we are nicely dressed and drinking a cup of tea. It's about that paradox as well. We are trapped in the processes of our own bodies – so it's a dirty protest. Nobody writes about having a shit every day but I'm sure people think about it much more than they admit. It's about imprisonment and freedom, and freedom from taboo. You can either see it as something positive or as something negative.

The paintings are also very abstract. It used to be a standard joke about abstract art, that it was something a child could do. But of course playing with their shit is exactly what some little children do.

It's to do with primary gesture. A child plays with its shit and then suddenly it has a moment of revulsion and starts to cry. It's seduced by the process and suddenly revolted by the material.

You've said that the material is always important to you, so it's presumably necessary for someone looking at this painting to know it's made of your own shit?

You tell me. It changes your perception when you do know. What I like is using the real material – you always find a poetry in it that you can never imagine. The real thing is always unexpected.

It's a bit like marble sculptures in that it makes you want to ask questions you would normally hesitate to ask, such as how did you actually do these paintings?

Well, I had a shit, smoothed it on the canvas, left it in the sun all day and then when it had dried I varnished the front which allows the shit to rehydrate. The back of the canvas is already varnished on the inside to prevent the moisture from leaking out.

The varnish gives it the look of an old master, as though it's badly in need of a clean.

I love the colour and the tone of it. It reminds me of a corner of a Rembrandt blown-up.

Did you have to dare yourself to do it?

In a way that's one of the interesting things about it. I kept thinking someone would come up and tell me to stop doing it.

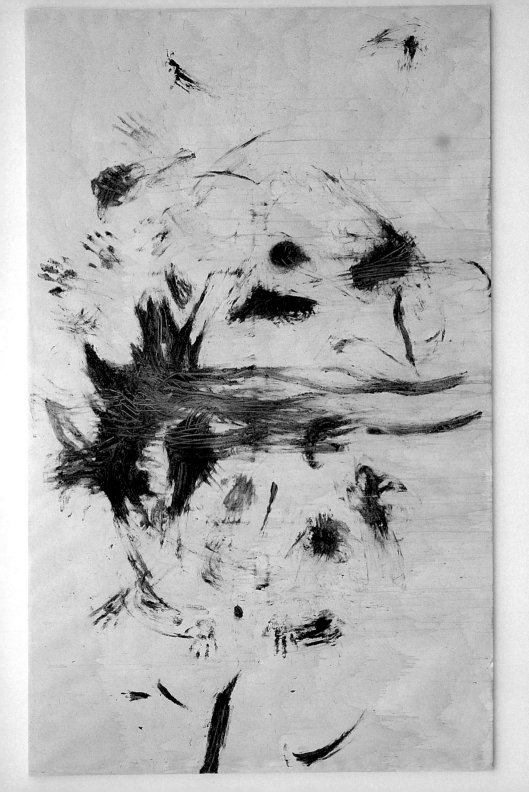

Shit Painting 28/8/97
1997
3600 x 2200
Artist's excrement
and resin on canvas
Jay Jopling/White Cube, London

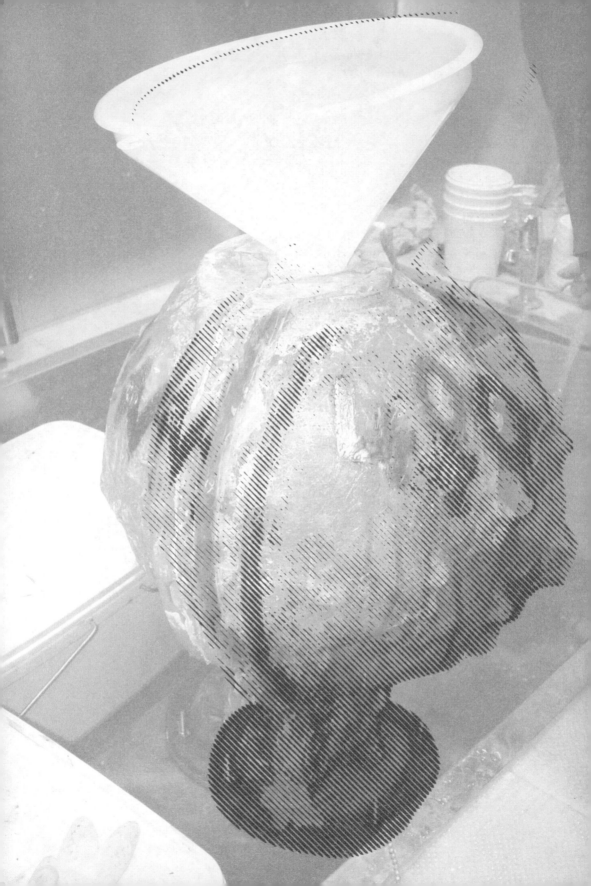

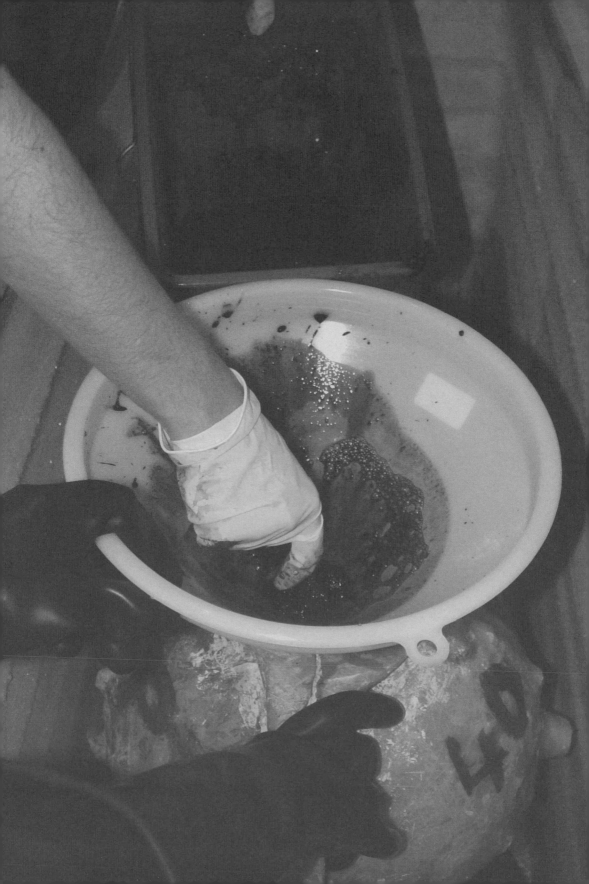

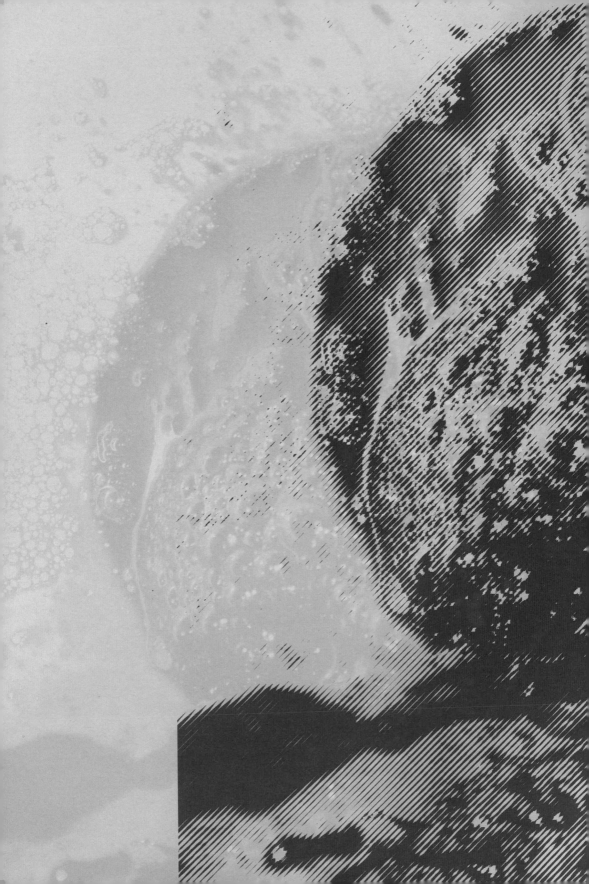

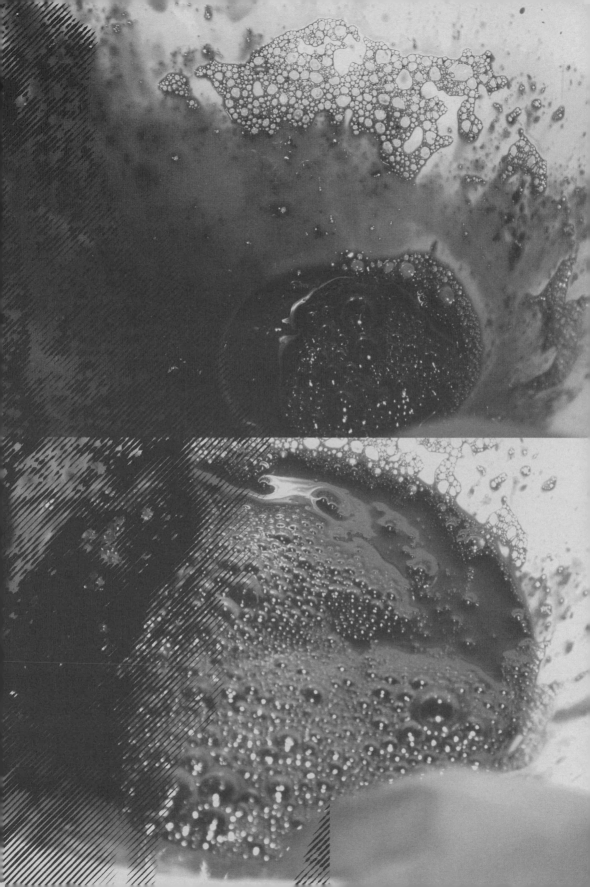

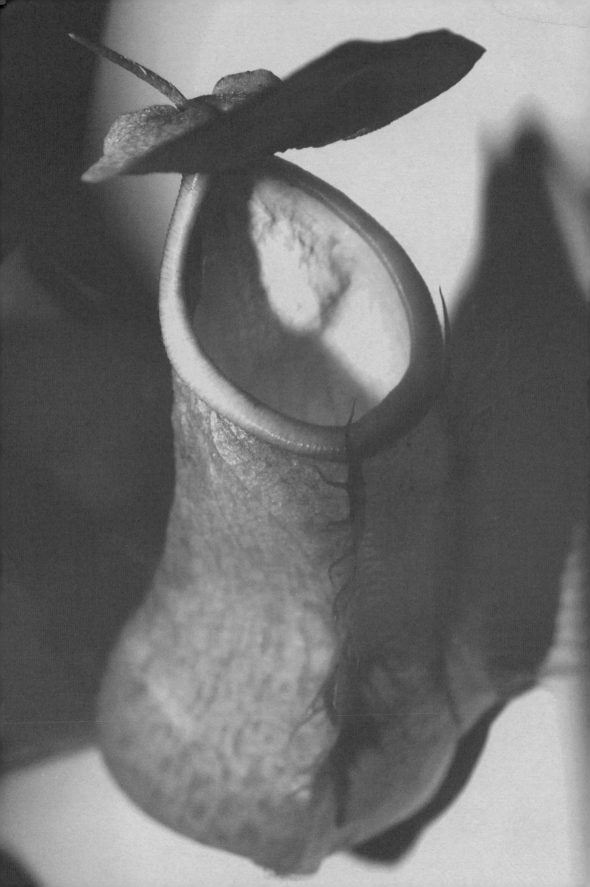

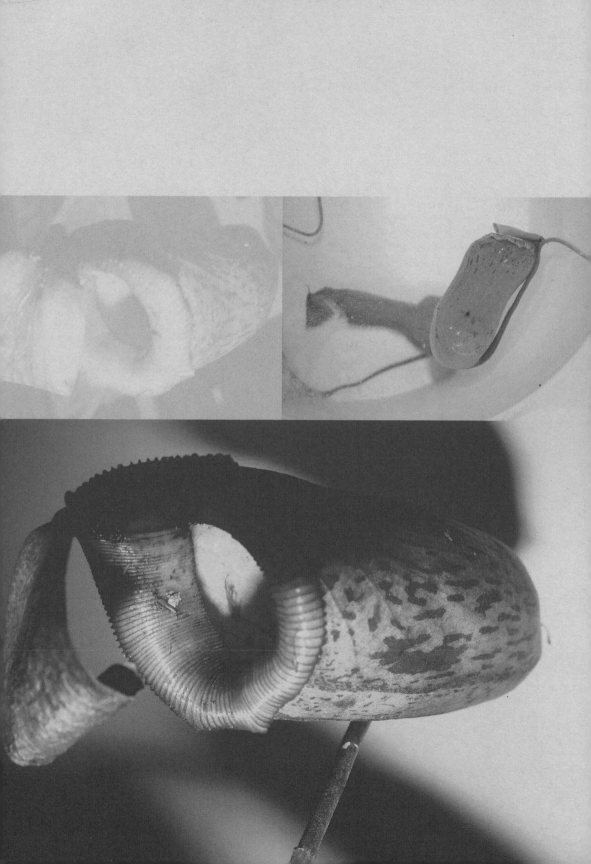

Flask
2002
2197 x 900 x 900
Stainless steel, glass, frozen silicone, blood, Nepenthes plant,
refrigeration equipment
Jay Jopling/White Cube, London

[11] The Flask

Sarah Whitfield — The way you use blood in your work seems to tie up with your love of polarities, that is to say, you make it appear both threatening and benign. Lucas's head is a benign object but *Flask* has a thoroughly sinister feel to it.

Marc Quinn — There is an implicit violence in all the blood sculptures. And it is right to read horror in *Flask* for example, more so than in the portrait heads. The flask is cast in animal blood and the flower, a Nepenthes, is carnivorous. It's a flower taken to the edge of its flowerness, an ordinary flower times a thousand. It's on such a level of extremeness, which is why I like it.

And it's fair to say that you take a particular pleasure in extremes?

That's what I do. I'm interested in all extremes. I like things that appear to strain at epitomising themselves.

You also seem to go out of your way to create an extreme situation. You told me earlier that making *Flask* was turning out to be typically nightmarish, and since we last spoke a few weeks ago you have had to postpone making the version with a Stapelia flower.

That's because the Stapelia flower comes into bloom too late for me to make that piece in time for this exhibition. I think it is an interesting flower because it's about the barriers of taxonomy. It simulates wounded flesh in order to attract the fly. It smells like death, ugliness and pain to us but it feels like beauty, desire and happiness to a fly. In the same way as when we look at a steak it's mouth-watering, delicious and nutritious but to a cow it's pain, unhappiness and death. Apparently the smell of rotting meat from the Stapelia flower is unbelievable. But there's the paradox. It stinks like death in order to procreate life. I will definitely make the work because I see the two flowers as a pair of sculptures that will work well together.

Both the Nepenthes and the Stapelia are flowers that have strikingly sculptural forms. The Nepenthes looks like an ancient vessel of some sort.

I love the way it is made, it has a beautiful structure. It looks like both the male and female sexual organs. The top looks like a vagina and the bottom like a penis, and it's hollow, like a vessel, as you say, so it also suggests a womb or a stomach. It's a site of transformation in which the body of the fly becomes plant as the plant sucks out its juices, so in a way it's like an inverse womb, sucking out life instead of creating it. It's the last piece in the show and a dark reflection of the first, *Lucas*, because the same kind of question can be asked. When does the fly cease to be fly and become plant? I find that moment as amazing and as moving as the creation of life. I am very interested in the idea that the physical world is made up of certain elements that are re-shaped in different ways. In this instance elements that were animal become plant. In the same way that when I die, the carbon atoms in my body will become a bit of dust or soot, if I'm burnt, and those atoms can circulate for a few thousand years and could eventually become a diamond. We are only contingent matrixes, we are not elemental. And there's another thing – the Nepenthes comes from the rainforest, so it relates back to the first room with the drawings, with all those pregnant possibilities and strange associations. It's nice to end the exhibition with a sculpture that relates back to the beginning.

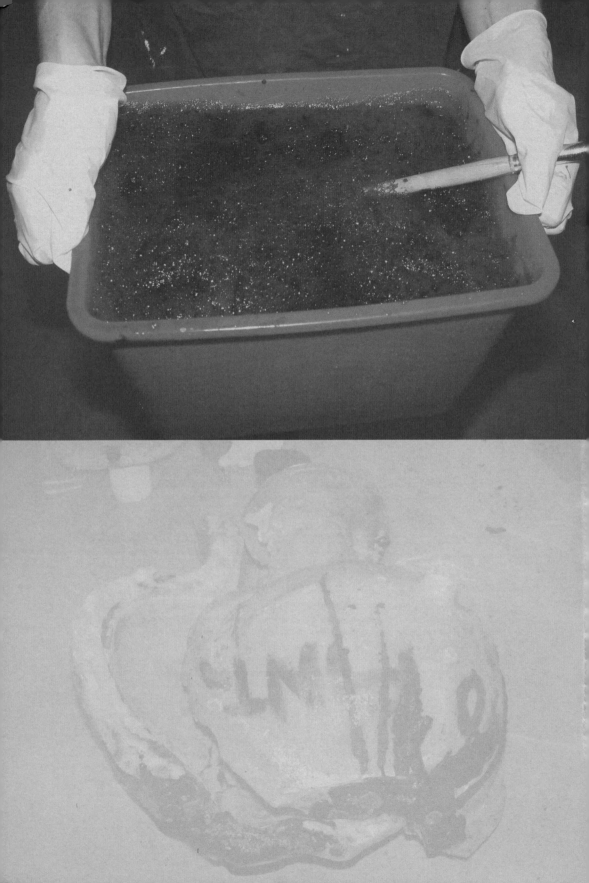

And the use of animal blood for the laboratory flask is another part of the transformation process I imagine?

The laboratory flask is another site of transformation, like a stomach. The work is about eating, digesting, and how in its brilliant way nature uses desire to make us do what it wants. And I used animal blood because I wanted to express the way we are abstracted from the reality. Meat is a product. It's an animal that has been killed but you go into a supermarket and you see these beautifully packaged pieces of meat. Society presents abstractions in order for it to continue. You can encourage a child to go and stroke a curly lamb and then feed it a lamb chop and no one sees any contradiction in that. That's how I got the idea of doing a Verner Panton chair in blood. When you see this chair you want to sit down in it, and by doing so you are immediately implicated in animal blood. Industrial design and industrial killing are both led by the same market desire. I like the abstraction of it.

You use blood very much as a fact of life. It's a subject we associate with martyrdoms and crucifixions, but not so much with the art of the last hundred years. Maybe that's because blood is too literal a subject for an age so used to visual metaphor?

Earlier art is much more to do with the real basic facts of life. When you are living in a medieval world there are only fundamental questions, there's no MTV. Art has to be of its own time. Rembrandt was about being a Dutch person in the seventeenth century but his painting still speaks to us now because there's some eternal aspect of the human condition that's epitomised in its moment. And if it hadn't been so real in its own time it wouldn't be so real now? That's the mystery, isn't it?

It is, you're right. Medieval painters believed in crucifixions. And unless something is a reality you are never going to make it with that conviction and belief. It has to be all or nothing, and it's that all or nothing that gives it a resonance that lasts.

Of course we find a lot of beauty in the horror of those early martyrdoms and crucifixions. And presumably you find a lot of beauty in blood or you wouldn't use it as a material?

One of the great things about making things out of frozen blood is the colour. When you see the sculptures in reality – you don't see this in a photograph – there is a kind of iridescence to the surface. It has a sparkly quality to it, a bit like the marble I used for the marble sculptures. It's horrific, but it's also deeply seductive.

All the frozen sculptures beg the question of permanence, which seems to be one of your major preoccupations.

What I love about the frozen pieces is creating a solidity that is completely contingent upon certain conditions. It's absolutely solid but it evokes the opposite. I wanted to make something about being alive, about life and death but in a purely sculptural form. When you turn the freezer off, however, the sculpture becomes a pool of blood and the form disappears. It's just not there. When I made the first blood head, I'd lost interest in art that was about art. I just wanted to make art that was about life. That is one thing I'm completely obsessed with – to make art that's about real life and not some hermetically sealed thing that's about itself.

Sarah Whitfield — Finally, does it interest you, or matter to you, how people look at your work?

Marc Quinn — It's very difficult for me to see how people look at it. It's one of the problems for an artist, especially when you are first starting to show your work. People make decisions about it based on their interpretation of it, which may be absolutely irrelevant to what you think about it, and the thing is, you'll never know.

And those decisions are often made in just a few seconds.

That's what I love about art. You have to devote a few hours to finding out whether a new novel is worth reading or not, whereas you can walk into an art gallery and know within one second whether you want to look further. There's the sense of the immediate moment, and of course, the longer you look, the more stuff seeps out.

In a way your work plays up to that.

Yes. I make things that can be grasped in a second but which are not what they seem. What I love about being an artist is that you have to live in the present moment. I suck in everything, watch TV, go to things, read books, magazines, talk to people, and then suddenly something clicks. I think that art should be accessible to people who don't think about it deeply, or talk about it, or live with it. You should be able to look at something even if you know nothing about the history of art, and have an immediate feeling or reaction to it. It's always about communication. It's a language, well, not really a language, it's an awareness, a form of non-verbal communication.

Isn't it also a question of the audience recognising their own reality in your reality? Everybody lives in a contemporary world, so if you have an art set in that world you will recognise something in it. Art is necessary for us, and the ambition of great art should be to do the job of philosophy and theology and work out just what it is to be a person in the world. There's so much richness to it. You can't de-invent experience, that's why you have to embrace life. You can't go back.

Marc Quinn: Art about Life
by Victoria Pomery

For more than ten years, Marc Quinn has been the main subject of his art and that is probably why I feel I recognise him. Quinn's studio is clean and organised, in fact it looks more like a living space than I had anticipated. Shelves of books, a sofa, a gleaming stainless steel stove and the sound of music filling the air. Closer inspection, however, suggests a room reminiscent of a laboratory, with its white walls, white-topped tables and the white chest freezer in the corner. The orderliness and sense of calm is palpable.

The far wall is covered in an array of drawings and photographs which relate to his most recent work. Organised into themes they too evoke the laboratory as much as the studio. There are images of Lucas, Quinn's son, of Alison Lapper and Parys modelling for the marble sculptures of mother and child, and studies for *Kiss*. The large format of some of these works is redolent of posters. This wall operates as a storyboard although there is nothing linear or circular about the arrangement of images – the works on the wall are an investigation of ideas, the notes for and of the experiments.

For Quinn drawing is an integral part of his practice; it is something he enjoys doing for its own sake and he tries to set aside time to draw every day. It is also a means of working through his ideas and of developing new ones. There are boxes of drawings housed in a cupboard on the other side of the studio and these are just a fraction of Quinn's total output. Each work is signed, dated and interleaved with a piece of acid-free tissue. As he and I leaf through the boxes, deciding what to include in the exhibition at Tate Liverpool and what to leave out, lines of enquiry emerge. The content of the work falls into themes, and there are groups which explore collage, others which involve burning or tearing the paper, some in pencil, others in crayon, ink or watercolour. The preciousness of these works lies in their ability to act as clues. Quinn's practice is all about enquiry, about the mystery and magic of life. His drawings hint at this – the repetition and exploration of imagery, the delight in the process, the abandonment with which marks are made.

Much has been made of the crossover between art and science in Quinn's work and in his background; his father is a scientist, his mother an artist. Both the terms 'art' and 'science' serve as shorthand for what are sometimes regarded as polarities, as incompatible disciplines unable to mix or borrow from one another. As the eminent scientist Stephen Jay Gould has remarked: 'Art and science are different enterprises, but the boundaries between them remain far more fluid and interdigitating, and the interactions far richer and more varied, than the usual stereotypes proclaim'.[1] Quinn manages to fuse the disciplines, to be creative in his use of new technology, materials and experimentation whilst referencing the history of art.

Throughout history there are countless examples of the crossover between art and science. I particularly enjoy that of the search to discover the manufacturing properties for porcelain in Europe in the early eighteenth century. This was a quest for beauty involving monetary gain, political intrigue and the transformation of materials. Chemists perfected the composition of the body, glazes and firing temperatures to

1
Gould, Stephen Jay,
*Leonardo's Mountain
of Clams and the Diet of
Worms*. London, Vintage,
1999, p45.

enable artists to produce beautiful, highly valued objects. The relationship was symbiotic. In many ways Quinn's mode of operation has similarities with the quest for porcelain or 'white gold' in that he plays the role of alchemist. It is a determined approach to find out more, to understand the properties of materials and to create.

Much of Quinn's recent work not only makes use of new technologies but also considers in some depth the role that science plays in the modern era. Quinn has remarked:

'I am very interested in scientific progress. The most progressive theories no longer deal with abstract questions of the subatomic structure and the like, but with problems of how our bodies are formed and developed. The research into genes, the structure of living cells and morphogenesis of various organs investigates things that interest me as an artist as well: the transformation of substance into a living body. The scientific avant-garde does concentrate today on the conditions of being. They deal with the same questions that are central to my work.[2]

His portrait of Sir John Sulston, commissioned by the National Portrait Gallery, is an example of Quinn's approach. Borrowing from the tradition of portraiture, he produces what could be regarded the truest likeness of the subject. Sulston, a leading contributor to the Human Genome project has commented: 'The portrait was made by our standard methods for DNA cloning. My DNA was broken randomly into segments, and treated so that they could be replicated in bacteria. The bacteria containing the DNA segments were spread out on agar jelly in the plate you see in the portrait.[3] Quinn has made a number of other works using this technique including his *Family Portrait (Cloned DNA)* 2001. Unlike the paintings of aristocratic family groups by Reynolds, Wright or Gainsborough in the eighteenth century in which the mise en scène is all important, these portraits are stripped to their barest essentials. The highly polished stainless steel frames emphasise the precious contents of these works and their reflective surface also operates as a mirror. These images are not only the truest form of portraiture but, in a contradictory way, the most universal. This is emphasised further in Quinn's *DNA Garden* 2001, a contemporary version of Adam and Eve in the Garden of Eden, a subject with a rich and long history in the tradition of image making.

Quinn's knowledge of and enthusiasm for the work of painters and sculptors throughout history informs his practice. There is nothing slavish about how he references genres or particular artists in his work – he is much more concerned about play and transformation when creating the work. Quinn's marble sculptures are a good case in point. In these works, he takes on some large issues not only relating to the history of sculpture but also to ideas and ideals about beauty and disability. Early Greek and Roman sculptures presented an idealised view of the body – athletic, perfectly proportioned, heroic types. Because of their great age, many of these works are no longer intact – a head missing here, a hand there. In 2000 Quinn presented a number of his pristine marble sculptures of both men and women in the sculpture galleries at the V&A in London. The combination of the new with the old, the gleaming with the tarnished was an unsettling experience and was much more about the process of working and the appearance of the material than the

2
In Jones, Jonathan, 'Portrait of the Week'. *The Guardian Saturday Review*, London, 22 September 2001, p4.

3
Lüdeking, Karlheinz 'Marc Quinn. What it means to be a living, material being'. *Kunstforum International*, Bonn, no. 148, December 1999, pp. 182–192.

subjects. Quinn works with models with disabilities, many of whom are artists in their own right. He intends the images to be positive and celebratory. A number of Quinn's sculptures can be seen at the Walker in Liverpool alongside nineteenth century sculptures that reference the antique but are several steps removed from those in the British Museum from which Quinn took his initial inspiration.

Quinn's work skilfully plays with opposites in the same way that he manages to bring together and pull apart art and science. In *Self*, a work which he makes a new version of every five years, Quinn uses his own blood to make a cast of his head. He has taken this a step further in the new work *Lucas* 2001 which is a cast of a modelled head of his new born son made from his placenta. The viewer is seduced by the beauty of the form and the surface of the blood, which crystallises when frozen, yet at the same time is repulsed by his use of such a material. Blood, like faeces and marble, has both symbolic and literal associations and Quinn uses these associations to explore the polarities of inside/outside, natural/artificial, seduction/repulsion and also the points at which such polarities collide.

It was with *Self* that Quinn first made use of refrigeration techniques – out of necessity at first and subsequently as a means of exploring immortality so that the pieces should be preserved forever. Since the first version of *Self* in 1991 Quinn has made a whole range of different works which utilise refrigeration. These have included such pieces as *Eternal Spring(Sunflowers)* I 1998 a bunch of sunflowers which also alludes to Van Gogh's paintings; *Love is All Around You* 1999 an evaporating frozen sculpture of lovers embracing; and his monumental *Garden* 2000. In these works, Quinn arranges flowers, often of the same variety, in a vase which is placed into a vitrine. His choice of flora is deliberate and includes lilies, sunflowers and orchids – all are exotic and many have symbolic associations, some are gaudy in colour or have erotic undertones. Once positioned in the vitrine, the natural cycle of life followed by death is suspended forever – the flower relinquishes its life for immortality. In *Garden* Quinn creates an entire other world in which all the plants are at the same point of perfection. Rather like the Dutch flower painters of the seventeenth century who painted large vases of flowers, none of which could have possibly been in bloom at the same time, Quinn is able to bring different elements together. Like them, the meaning of *Garden* is far more than a cornucopia of nature's riches; it is a piece in which the fragility of life and the finality of death are played out.

As the daylight fades we complete the task of selecting the drawings. It has been an exhausting process, crouching on the floor, considering each work. My mind is full of an accumulation of images, all craving my attention. A drawing of a male torso with the internal workings of his body revealed makes a particular impression. It looks a bit like a diagram in a biology text book or on the wall of a classroom. It reiterates the polarities of inside and outside, that we exist in the world but that the interior workings of body and mind are ingenious. Quinn's work constantly pursues the how, who and what we are in the world. His exhibition at Tate Liverpool presents an opportunity to consider his practice afresh. The large gallery spaces allow fluid readings of the work, to reveal no real answers but plenty of challenging questions.

Marc Quinn – List of works
Dimensions in millimetres,
Height x width x depth
* Located at the Walker

1989 – 2002
Selection of approx. 150
Drawings and C-type prints
Dimensions variable
Various media
Courtesy of the artist and Jay
Jopling/White Cube, London

1996
No Visible Means of Escape IV
4000 x 600 x 400
R.T.V. polyurethene
Tate

The Etymology of Morphology
270 x 1525 x 1520
Glass and silver
Tate

1997
Shit Painting 28/8/97
3600 x 2200
Artist's excrement
and resin on canvas
Jay Jopling/White Cube, London

1998
Eternal Spring (Lilies) II
2197 x 900 x 900
Stainless steel, glass,
frozen silicone, lilies,
refrigeration equipment
Private Collection, London

**Study for Approaching Planck
Density 64.5 Kg**
670 x 440 x 130
Cast lead
Courtesy of the artist

**Study for Approaching Planck
Density 71 Kg**
102 x 534 x 356
Cast lead
Courtesy of the artist

**Study for Approaching Planck
Density 82.75 Kg**
570 x 500 x 150
Cast lead
Courtesy of the artist

1999
Coaxial Planck Density
1860 x 520 x 120
Cast lead
Jay Jopling/White Cube, London

Peter Hull*
840 x 480 x 380
Marble
Private Collection, Liverpool

2000
Alison Lapper & Parys
835 x 435 x 620
Marble
Mugrabi Collection

Alison Lapper (8 Months)
835 x 400 x 650
Marble
Mugrabi Collection

Catherine Long*
1590 x 500 x 740
Marble
Jay Jopling/White Cube, London

Helen Smith*
900 x 700 x 620
Marble
Courtesy of the artist

Italian Landscape 3
1098 x 1663 x 42
Permanent pigment on canvas
Jay Jopling/White Cube, London

Italian Landscape 5
1098 x 1663 x 42
Permanent pigment on canvas
Jay Jopling/White Cube, London

Italian Landscape 6
1098 x 1663 x 42
Permanent pigment on canvas
Jay Jopling/White Cube, London

Italian Landscape 10
1098 x 1663 x 42
Permanent pigment on canvas
White Cube

Painting by Numbers
1098 x 1663 x 42
Permanent pigment, acrylic
and Letraset on canvas
Jay Jopling/White Cube, London

Self Conscious
190 x 120 x 275
Glass, perspex, 90% alcohol and
human DNA (Artist's)
Collezione Prada

2001
Reconstruction
1100 x 1660 x 50
Canvas, permanent pigment,
acrylic and letraset
Jay Jopling/White Cube, London

Reconstruction Site
1100 x 1660 x 50
Canvas, permanent pigment,
acrylic and letraset
Jay Jopling/White Cube, London

Reconstruction by Numbers
1110 x 1666 x 50
Canvas, permanent pigment,
acrylic and letraset
Jay Jopling/White Cube, London

2001 – 2002
Mirror Self Portrait
1988 x 1435
Mirror, stainless steel box frame
Jay Jopling/White Cube, London

2002
DNA Garden
1925 x 3260
Stainless steel frame,
polycarbonate agar jelly, bacteria
colonies, 77 plates of cloned
DNA – 75 plants, 2 humans
Jay Jopling/White Cube, London

Family Portrait (Cloned DNA)
262 x 205 x 27
Stainless steel, polycarbonate
agar jelly, bacteria colonies,
cloned human DNA
Jay Jopling/White Cube, London

Flask
2197 x 900 x 900
Stainless steel, glass, frozen
silicone, blood, Nepenthes plant,
refrigeration equipment
Jay Jopling/White Cube, London

Kiss
1759 x 640 x 600
Marble
Jay Jopling/White Cube, London

Lucas
2046 x 640 x 640
Human placenta and umbilical
cord, stainless steel, perspex,
refrigeration equipment
Jay Jopling/White Cube, London

96/0.3
1538 x 1025
Pigment print on gessoed board
Jay Jopling/White Cube, London

Biography

1964 Born in London
Lives and works in London

Solo Exhibitions
* indicates publication

2001
A Genomic Portrait: Sir John Sulston by Marc Quinn,
National Portrait Gallery, London

Marc Quinn: Garden
Art of this Century, Paris

Italian Landscape
Habitat, London

2000
Still Life
White Cube*, London

Marc Quinn
Groningen Museum, Holland

Marc Quinn
Fondazione Prada, Milan*

1999
Marc Quinn
Kunstverein Hannover*

Marc Quinn: Drawings
Sala Amárica-América Aretoa,
Victoria, Spain

1998
Marc Quinn: Incarnate
Gagosian Gallery, New York*

Marc Quinn
South London Gallery*

1997
Infra-slim Spaces
Invisible Museum, SCCA, Kiev

1995
Art Now – Emotional Detox: The Seven Deadly Sins
Tate Gallery, London*

The Blind Leading the Blind
Jay Jopling/White Cube, London

1994
Marc Quinn
Jay Jopling/Art Hotel Art Fair,
Amsterdam

1993
Marc Quinn
Galerie Jean Bernier, Athens

1991
Out of Time
Jay Jopling/Grob Gallery, London

1990
Bread Sculpture
Galerie Nikki Diana Marquardt,
Paris

Bread Sculpture
Middendorf Gallery, Washington

1988
Bronze Sculpture
Jay Jopling/Otis Gallery, London

Selected Group Exhibitions

2001
**Die Sammlung Olbricht, Teil 2.
Without Hesitation**
Gesellschaft für Aktuelle Kunst
and Neues Museum Weserburg,
Bremen

Metamorphosis and Cloning
Musée d'Art Contemporaine
de Montréal

Summer Exhibition 2001
Royal Academy of Arts, London*

Arts
Lux Gallery, London

London Nomad
Cairo Biennale

Mind the Gap
Wetterling Gallery, Stockholm*

Give & Take
Victoria & Albert Museum,
London

Heads and Hands
Decatur House Museum,
Washington

2000
Wellcome Wing
Science Museum, London

Conversation
Milton Keynes Art Gallery

**Spectacular Bodies: The Art and
Science of the Human Body
from Leonardo to Now**
Hayward Gallery, London*

Out There
White Cube*, London

Psycho
Anne Faggionato, London

1999
Skin
Deste Foundation Centre for
Contemporary Art, Athens*

Something Warm and Fuzzy
Des Moines Art Center

**Into the Light: Photographic
Printing Out of the Darkroom**
The Royal Photographic Society,
Bath

Officina Europa
Galleria d'Arte Moderna di
Bologna

**Now It's My Turn to Scream:
Works by Contemporary British
Artists from the Logan Collection**
Haines Gallery, San Francisco*

Presence
Tate Gallery Liverpool

**As Above, So Below:
The Body's Equal Parts**
Fabric Workshop, Philadelphia

**Spaced Out: Late 1990s Works
from the Vicki and Kent Logan
Collection,**
The CCA Institute, California*

Physical Evidence
Kettle's Yard, Cambridge

1998
**A Portrait of Our Times: An
Introduction to the Logan
Collection**
San Francisco Museum of
Modern Art*

UK Maximum Diversity
Galerie Krinzinger, Benger
Fabrik Bregenz, Austria*

Group exhibition
Galleri Faurschou, Copenhagen

Hope (Sufferance)
Sun and Doves Gallery, London

**The Colony Room 50th
Anniversary Art Exhibition**
A22 Projects, London

**Sam Taylor-Wood, Tracey Emin,
Gillian Wearing, Marc Quinn**
Galerija Dante Marino Cettina,
Umag, Croatia

Inner Self
Mitchell-Innes & Nash, New
York

1997
The Quick and the Dead:
Artists and Anatomy
Royal College of Art, London;
Mead Gallery, University of
Warwick; City Art Gallery, Leeds*

Follow Me
Kunstverein Kehdingen,
Freiburg, Germany*

Sensation: Young British Artists
from the Saatchi Collection
Royal Academy of Arts, London;
Hamburger Bahnhof, Berlin;
Brooklyn Museum of Art,
New York*

The Body
The Art Gallery of New South
Wales, Sydney*

A Ilha do Tesouro
Fundação Calouste Gulbenkian,
Lisbon*

1996
Thinking Print:
Books to Billboards 1980-95
Museum of Modern Art,
New York*

Hybrid
De Appel, Amsterdam

Feed and Greed
MAK: Austrian Museum of
Applied Arts, Vienna*

Works on Paper
Irish Museum of Modern Art,
Dublin

Happy End
Kunsthalle, Düsseldorf

1995
Time Machine
Museo Egizio, Turin

Faith, Hope, Charity
Kunsthalle, Vienna*

Contemporary British Art in
Print
Scottish Museum of Modern
Art, Edinburgh*

Ripple Across the Water
Minato Prefecture and Shibuya
Prefecture, Tokyo*

1994
Life is too Much
Galerie des Archives, Paris

Time Machine
British Museum, London

1993
Young British Artists II
Saatchi Gallery, London*

Prospect '93
Frankfurt*

Sonsbeek '93
Arnhem, Holland*

Real
Wiener Secession, Vienna*

Restaurant
Marc Jancou, Paris*

1992
London Portfolio
Karsten Schubert Ltd, London

Strange Developments
Anthony d'Offay Gallery,
London

British Art
Barbara Gladstone Gallery, New
York*

9th Sydney Biennale
Sydney*

1991
Modern Masters
Grob Gallery, London

1990
Group Show
Grob Gallery, London

Hands
Grob Gallery, London

Awards

2001
The Royal Academy of Arts
Charles Wollaston Award